Decorative
MURALS
with Donna Dewberry

DECORATIVE
MURALS
with DONNA DEWBERRY

NORTH LIGHT BOOKS
Cincinnati, Ohio

about the author

Donna Dewberry is an acclaimed decorative artist, teacher and author who has taken the one-stroke painting technique and made it her own. She shares her passion for painting with students all over the world via classes, seminars, books, videos and television appearances. Her previous book, *Donna Dewberry's Complete Book of One-Stroke Painting* (North Light Books, 1998), includes twelve dazzling step-by-step projects even beginners can paint easily and quickly.

Donna's husband, Marc, remembers the evening Donna began her decorative wall painting. "She was at our dining room table painting items for her gift shop. Apparently, during the night she ran out of surfaces and simply began painting on a wall. When I awoke the next morning, there was an entire scene painted on the wall. I must have encouraged her about how well she had done because the next thing I knew she was painting on every wall and door in our home. I think out of survival instincts I told her that it wasn't fair we were the only ones who had decorative painting on our walls and she should paint on some of our friends' walls as well. She did just that and today she has painted in over 1,200 homes and businesses. I am thankful to be part of her life, and I recognize her talent and envy her passion."

Decorative Murals with Donna Dewberry. Copyright © 1999 by Donna Dewberry. Manufactured in Singapore. All rights reserved. The patterns and drawings in this book are for the personal use of the decorative painter. By permission of the author and publisher, they may be either hand-traced or photocopied to make single copies, but under no circumstances may they be resold or republished. It is permissible for the purchaser to paint the designs contained herein and sell them at fairs, bazaars and craft shows. No other part of this book may be reproduced in any form or by any electronic or mechanical means including information storage and retrieval systems without permission in writing from the publisher, except by a reviewer, who may quote brief passages in a review. Published by North Light Books, an imprint of F&W Publications, Inc., 4700 East Galbraith Road, Cincinnati, Ohio 45236. (800) 289-0963. First edition.

Other fine North Light Books are available from your local bookstore, art supply store or direct from the publisher.

07 06 05 04 03   14 13 12 11 10

Library of Congress Cataloging-in-Publication Data

Dewberry, Donna S.
    Decorative murals with Donna Dewberry / Donna Dewberry.—1st ed.
        p.   cm.
    Includes index.
    ISBN 0-89134-988-X (pbk.: alk. paper)
    1. Acrylic painting-Technique. 2. Mural painting and decoration. I. Title.
TT385.D475   1999
751.7'3—dc21   98-53826
                                                                                        CIP

Editor: Kathy Kipp
Associate Editors: Amy J. Wolgemuth and Christine Doyle
Production Coordinator: Erin Boggs
Designer: Mary Barnes Clark
Photographer: Jerry Mucklow

Jerry Mucklow is a commercial photographer based in Atlanta, Georgia, with over seventeen years of professional experience. For the past three years Jerry has been the Senior Staff Photographer with Phoenix Communications, photographing on location as well as shooting product in the studio with cutting edge digital technology.

dedication

We all have dreams, but for many of us, dreams may never become reality. I have been blessed to have had many of my dreams come true. The Lord blessed me with the man of my dreams. I fell deeply in love with my husband, Marc, in high school and we've been married for twenty-six years. As a parent, Marc is a wonderful example for our seven children, always sacrificing and giving of himself.

Many years ago, Marc had faith in my desire to become an interior decorator, own a gift shop, sculpt, paint wall murals and manufacture giftware. And now he has faith in my desire to be published, to design a line of how-to-paint products and teach courses that help others make their dreams come true.

Marc has worked side by side with me, selling, shipping, accounting, producing and completely taking care of the things I didn't want to so I could just create! Marc thinks he doesn't know how to paint, but he has gained great insight by being there with me as I've created my brushstrokes and designs. He knows how to explain them to beginners and those who are unfamiliar with strokework and painting terminology.

When I was discouraged and wanted to give up, Marc inspired me. His help and support have made my ultimate dream come true: this book—a showcase of some of the many homes in which I've painted my designs and a guide for anyone who wants to decorate their own homes and furniture easily and quickly.

I dedicate this book to Marc, my eternal companion. He knows I still have many more dreams to fulfill, and I know he'll figure out how to help make those happen for me, too.

Marc, I love you for being my friend, husband, father of our children and the man you are!

table of contents

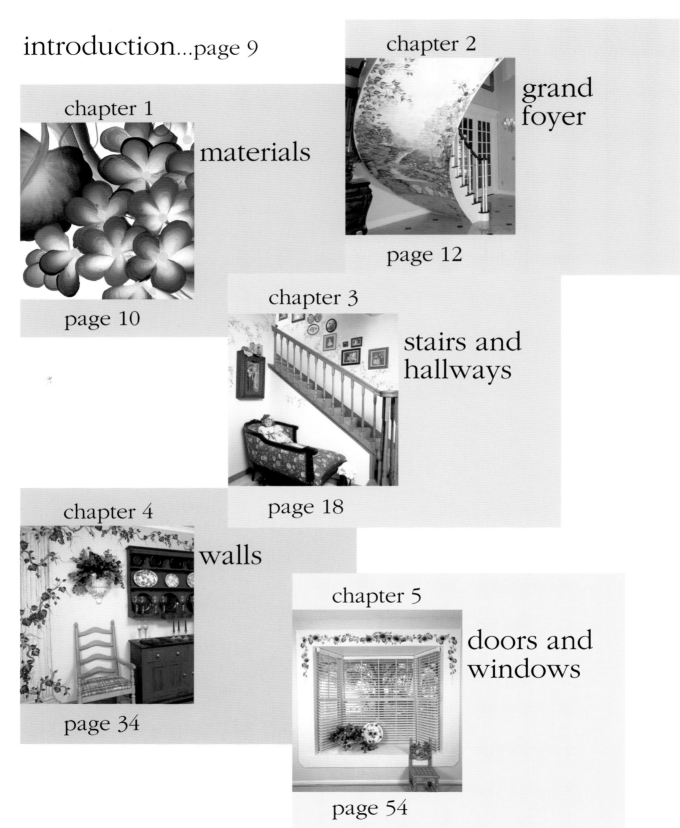

introduction...page 9

chapter 1

materials

page 10

chapter 2

grand foyer

page 12

chapter 3

stairs and hallways

page 18

chapter 4

walls

page 34

chapter 5

doors and windows

page 54

chapter 6

living
and
family
rooms

page 72

chapter 7

kitchens
and
dining
rooms

page 90

chapter 8

laundry
rooms

page 106

chapter 9

bathrooms

page 112

chapter 10

bedrooms

page 128

index...page 144

acknowledgments

As in the case of all books, there are many people who may not receive the recognition or thanks they deserve. I would like to recognize those who have helped make this book a reality. Hopefully, I will not forget anyone.

First, a huge thank you to all of the wonderful people who shared their homes with me and asked me to come in and paint. Thanks to Hank, Nikki and Mary Ann Nieroda and Domino (the dog), to Steve and Kathryn Lowery, and to Laurel Matheson. You are very gracious and kind, and I am delighted to know each of you!

Second, thanks to my brother, Jerry, for his assistance with the staircase in the Lowery home. He is a talented artist and I wish him the best in his endeavors. Special thanks to Jerry Mucklow, who did all the photography in this book and was patient, kind and considerate. To all the people at North Light Books—I know it takes a lot of time and hard work to publish a book. I am grateful to each of you.

Last, but not least, I would like to convey my deep sense of gratitude to a very special person who has become a lifelong friend. Kathy Kipp, my editor, has been great to work with. She is honest but kind, serious but fun, faces reality but is ever imaginative and patient with me and my artistic sensibilities. She has always been positive, even when things seemed otherwise. Kathy, it is people like you who make all of this possible. Thank you.

introduction

This book is the result of a lot of hard work and a lifelong dream to share some of my ideas and my passion for decorative wall and furniture painting. I hope this book will inspire a desire within each of you to paint not only with excitement, but also total confidence in yourself and your creative abilities.

I clearly recall how unsure and nervous I was the first time I touched a paintbrush to a wall. As I painted, I began to feel less nervous, and there were moments when I felt almost adventurous. I let myself become more relaxed and comfortable, and as I did, I realized that my painting was taking on a new meaning. I was actually expressing some of my creative talent (or, should I say, I was discovering that I actually had some), and the more I painted, the less anxious I felt.

To date, I have painted over 1,200 decorative projects in homes and businesses. I have painted on just about every type of surface there is—indoors and outdoors; on walls, ceilings and floors; and around doors and every other opening you can imagine. The one thing that remains constant is that no two painting projects are ever alike—you can create something new for every situation. I guess that is what all artistic people want—to be able to create and never repeat the same thing twice.

I hope that what I share with you will not only give you many ideas, but will encourage you to be adventuresome. Let your creative talents guide you, and paint with enthusiasm. With each stroke, your confidence will grow and you will venture into the world of decorative painting like you never have before. If I can share just one more thought with you, it is this: Remember, I may have painted on a lot of walls, but I began on one.

Editor's Note: The decorative painting projects in this book were created and photographed in actual homes, not in a slick and sterile set of a photographer's studio. The families that live in these homes have left their mark. The occasional scratch, fingerprint and dusty corner remind us that beautiful artwork on the walls can not only coexist comfortably with our busy everyday lives, but enrich and enhance them as well.

chapter 1

materials

Brushes

The brushes I used to create all the artwork in this book are called One-Stroke by Plaid. The nylon bristles of the flat brushes are longer and a little thinner than other brushes so that as I do my brushstrokes, they spring back up to the chisel edge. I do most of my strokework with synthetic flat brushes because they keep a nicer chisel edge. I use two sizes of the script liner for detail. The One-Stroke script liners have more and longer bristles that hold more paint longer than other brushes. The scruffy brushes, made with natural hair bristles, are soft with a lot of bounce. They're not like deerfoot or stippler brushes, which are stiffer.

Brushes

All of the projects in this book were done with these few One-Stroke brushes from Plaid: a ¾-inch flat, no. 12 flat, no. 2 script liner, small scruffy brush, large scruffy brush and, in the package, no. 2 and no. 6 flats and a no. 1 script liner. You can find these brushes at any craft or art supply store.

Supplies

Most of my painting supplies are inexpensive and can be found around the house. For example, I use plain white styrofoam plates as my palette because the paint doesn't dry up and absorb into the plates, and their light weight makes them easier to hold for a long time.

The big sponge I use is a car wash-type sponge you can buy at a hardware or auto supply store. I use it to add faux finishes to walls and furniture.

A water basin is important for protecting your brushes and the rake at the bottom makes it easier to clean flat brushes. The basin I use has holes along the edge that hold my brushes so the tips of the bristles don't bend, and it separates the clean from dirty water.

I use paper towels for general cleanup and to dry my brushes for color changes. The sponge roller makes applying base coats quicker and easier. Most hardware or paint supply stores have them.

I prefer a spray matte sealer when painting on furniture. It has a low luster that gives the piece a high-quality look. I use FolkArt's Clearcote Hi-Shine Glaze on metal and pieces that are already shiny or glossy. Neither of these are needed on walls because the acrylic paints I use are completely washable.

Paints and Mediums

I use FolkArt acrylic paints exclusively because they're thick and creamy and have so many good colors that I rarely have to mix my own. For large projects, you might want to purchase the eight-ounce bottles, but the two-ounce bottles go a long way.

I use FolkArt's Crackle Medium because it's a no-fail method: All the stages of crackling are in one medium. FolkArt's Floating Medium, mixed with paint, is great for shading, and the Antiquing Medium gives a warm, soft, old-world look, even to brand-new pieces. It's water-based, so you can easily rub it on and off.

Water-based varnish comes in several lusters, but I prefer the satin. It comes in exterior varnishes, too. I love using water-based varnish on pieces that will get a lot of wear, such as tables and floorcloths, because it's a hardier finish than a spray sealer.

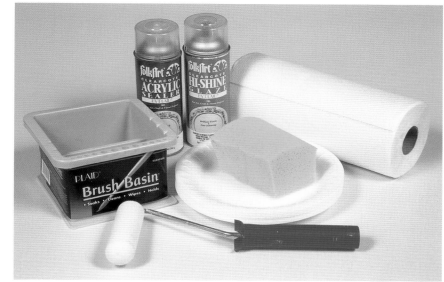

Miscellaneous Supplies
The only other supplies I use include paper towels; styrofoam plates; a large, car wash-type sponge; a water container; and occasionally a spray acrylic sealer, glaze and a small sponge roller.

Paints and Mediums
FolkArt acrylic paints come in such a wide array of colors that I seldom need to mix my own. Certain colors that I use a lot, such as Honeycomb and Linen, I buy in large eight-ounce bottles. I also use Crackle Medium, Antiquing Medium and Water-based Varnish by FolkArt.

chapter 2

grand foyer

surface: smooth plaster

The entrance to a house, whether a grand foyer like this one or a simple front door, makes an indelible first impression if it's personalized with a painted design that's appropriate in size and style. This two-story foyer included a long, curving staircase, a wall of gilt-framed mirrors and a marble floor. The foyer led directly to the formal living room, and anyone sitting in the living room could see the plain white back of the freestanding staircase. Therefore, the homeowner wanted a dramatic yet tasteful design that would lead the eye up the back of the staircase, across the ceiling and down the wall, ending in a French niche. The colors had to harmonize with the whites, creams and browns of the foyer.

This project was a large undertaking with many challenges. To avoid being overwhelmed, I broke it down into small parts and concentrated on each part, painting a layer at a time and building outward with detail.

MATERIALS USED

Brushes:
¾-inch flat
nos. 2, 6 and 12 flats
no. 2 script liner
scruffy brush

Miscellaneous:
Floating Medium
Natural sea sponge

Paint Colors:

Alizarin Crimson	Basil Green	Bayberry	Berry Wine
Burnt Sienna	Burnt Umber	Butter Pecan	Dioxazine Purple
Green Forest	Heartland Blue	Maple Syrup	Maroon
Midnight	Night Sky	Olive Green	Rose Garden
Sunflower	Tapioca	Thicket	Twill
Wicker White			

Detail of Staircase Ceiling

I began the project with a faux blue-sky-and-clouds effect (more like a very subtle wash) for the entire overhead section of the staircase and continued down the back of the upper part of the staircase. For the lower part, I painted a soft green wash for the first layer of the scene.

On the ceiling area, I painted in the trellis with Basil Green and Bayberry with a little Wicker White.

Pencilling in a pattern for accuracy helped to get the latticework even. Then I painted all of the vines, carrying them down to the lower part of the staircase. I used Floating Medium and, alternating Basil, Bayberry and Thicket greens, I added the leafing.

To finish, I added roses in two shades: Maroon and Butter Pecan for the darker roses, and Rose Garden and Wicker White for the lighter pink ones.

Detail of Scene

This scene gives the impression that the viewer is on a porch looking out over a brook, a pathway and an arched bridge. The horizon line of the scene is actually at eye level. The trees and vines were painted to appear closer to the viewer, adding depth of field to the scene. The foreground vines were carried up the staircase and joined to the more subtly colored vines overhead.

I started the scene by painting the stones in the porch, then based in the water that flows away from the porch. Using the same tones—Butter Pecan, Maple Syrup, Wicker White and Twill (none of which are gray)—I painted in the columns, railings and urn, then the road and bridge and finally the trees

in the background. On the pathway and arched bridge, I added some Burnt Sienna.

I used my scruffy brush and little pieces of natural sea sponges to moss in the foliage of the trees, background greenery and ground cover. Then I added little hints of flower colors. I also added touches of those colors to the water for reflections, being sure to paint in the bridge's reflection as well. To give the effect of reflections, I painted subtle white streaks *over* the reflections of the flowers and greenery.

To finish, I detailed the bricks, small vines on the bridge, moss and cracks on the porch and rails, and vines draping out of the urn.

French Niche

On the opposite side of the foyer from the curving staircase is a French urn niche. Above the niche is the ceiling created by the staircase, shown on page 14. To connect all the elements of the foyer, I continued the ceiling's rose and vine pattern down the wall and into the niche itself, shaping the vine to frame the brass urn and create a focal point.

The walls had been painted in Buttercream and the niche and moldings were white. To keep the rose and vine pattern soft, airy and subtle, I painted in a lot of shadow leaves using Floating Medium and Basil Green, Thicket and Butter Pecan.

Detail of Niche

I used the chisel edge of a ¾-inch flat brush double-loaded with Burnt Umber and Butter Pecan to paint all of the vines first. Then I painted all of the lighter pink roses using Rose Garden and Wicker White, and the darker roses with Maroon and Butter Pecan.

I painted the most subtle shadow leafing with Floating Medium, Basil Green and Butter Pecan. To finish, I used Thicket and Butter Pecan for the darker leaves, and inky Thicket for the curlicue vines.

chapter 3

stairs and hallways

surface: painted walls

The walls of staircases and hallways can be great places to do decorative painting. The long, empty expanses provide plenty of room to experiment with any number of design ideas, from trailing vines or florals to entire landscapes. Family members can personalize the hallways outside of their rooms, and as the children grow, the designs can change and grow with them.

It's fun to put a gallery of family photos on a staircase wall, and a twining vine helps tie the photos together. The family who lived in the house shown at right had old and new photos in many different-shaped frames, plus some interesting antique furniture, dolls and clothing. I worked with the homeowner to design a trailing vine of rosebuds and leaves that would be subtle and delicate enough not to detract from the antiques and family pictures.

First we arranged the pictures up the staircase wall in groupings that complemented the frames and portraits. Then I painted around and between the frames in a graceful, flowing manner that softened the edges of the square frames and tied the oval frames together.

The vine was painted with Maple Syrup and Wicker White double-loaded on a ¾-inch flat brush. I started at the bottom of the stairs and wound up and around the pictures all the way to the top. Occasionally I trailed the vine away from the pictures. I also pulled the vine motif into the foyer by winding it down and around antique pieces in the room. I went back with a no. 12 flat brush double-loaded with Rose Chiffon and Wicker White and painted mostly double clusters of wild roses. I finished with green one-stroke leaves and curlicues in Green Forest and Wicker White.

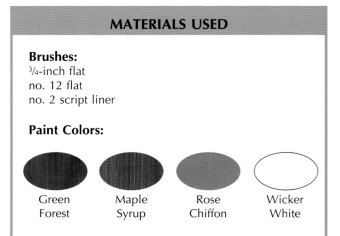

MATERIALS USED			
Brushes: ¾-inch flat, no. 12 flat, no. 2 script liner			
Paint Colors:			
Green Forest	Maple Syrup	Rose Chiffon	Wicker White

Family Tree and House Signs

surface: hallway wall

Hallways like this one at the top of the stairs are often too narrow to hang pictures or put furniture, but what a great place to paint a floor-to-ceiling mural! A tree with a flower-bedecked swing and a house sign with twining morning glories fit this wall beautifully, and the garden colors helped dress up an otherwise plain hallway.

The tree is a nice surprise that becomes visible as you go up the stairs. The family wanted a multipurpose tree: It not only has a swing and a hat with ribbons, but is also a "family tree." The large leaves are painted with the parents' names and the small leaves with the children's. Each side of the family has its own side of the tree and, most touchingly, deceased family members have a rosebud painted by their names. Leaves can be added as the family grows—it becomes a living genealogy.

The vines on the swing were enhanced with little clusters of wisteria. The ribbons on the hat were painted with a no. 12 flat brush double-loaded with Wicker White and Midnight before the flowers and leaves were added.

The house signs and posts were painted to give a trompe l'oeil effect. I basecoated most of the signs with a sponge, then shaded them with a flat brush. Morning glories growing up the main sign-post were painted with Midnight and Wicker White. I added a hummingbird hovering around the blossoms. The sign tells when the family was established.

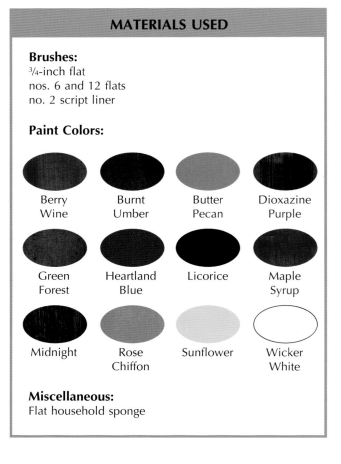

MATERIALS USED

Brushes:
3/4-inch flat
nos. 6 and 12 flats
no. 2 script liner

Paint Colors:

Berry Wine

Burnt Umber

Butter Pecan

Dioxazine Purple

Green Forest

Heartland Blue

Licorice

Maple Syrup

Midnight

Rose Chiffon

Sunflower

Wicker White

Miscellaneous:
Flat household sponge

Rose Trellis and Wall Plaque

surface: hallway wall

This hallway leads from the girls' bedroom into their bathroom, and the wall is broken up by a narrow offset. That gave me two distinct but adjoining "canvases" on which to paint. The chosen designs—a vining trellis and a wall plaque—used roses as their common element.

The latticework trellis and vine were painted with Burnt Umber and Wicker White on the chisel edge of a ¾-inch flat brush. Green leaves and vines (Green Forest and Wicker White), rosebuds (Berry Wine and Wicker White) and butterflies (Yellow Ochre and Wicker White) were added, with one trailing vine leading over to the adjacent wall.

Next to the linen closet in the girls' bathroom, I painted a trompe l'oeil table with a candle, basket of yarn and a chubby little angel sitting on a lace-edged pillow. The bathroom wall has a painted border of vines with soft pink trailing flowers.

The pink wall plaque was personalized with the girls' grandmother's name, Rose, and was hung with a big, blue painted ribbon.

MATERIALS USED

Brushes:
¾-inch flat
nos. 2, 6 and 12 flats
nos. 1 and 2 script liners
scruffy brush

Paint Colors:

Berry Wine	Burnt Umber	Butter Pecan	Green Forest
Maple Syrup	Midnight	Rose Garden	Wicker White
Yellow Ochre			

Miscellaneous:
Flat household sponge

Garden Cart

surface: hallway walls

This hallway at the top of a stairway joined together two children's bedrooms, so the family wanted a design that included colorful motifs that kids enjoy—sunshine, clouds, bunnies, squirrels, butterflies and bumblebees. I painted a realistic-looking squirrel leaving nuts on top of the door jamb. A bright sun was painted with Sunflower and Yellow Ochre. Blue and white billowy clouds were painted using a sponge. Over a collage of the little girl's photo and her baby clothes, a spray of yellow roses and green leaves was added. Underneath the collage, I painted a wisteria vine and gardenia bush.

On the wall facing the stairs, an old wooden garden cart spilling over with flowers leads the eye to a flower-covered bench. The cart has geraniums, violets, bougainvillea and goldenrod. Under the cart are wildflowers, and a spotted bunny sits among the grass.

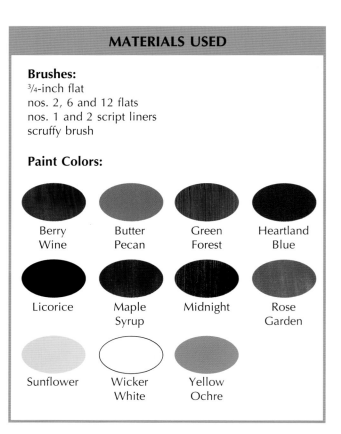

MATERIALS USED

Brushes:
¾-inch flat
nos. 2, 6 and 12 flats
nos. 1 and 2 script liners
scruffy brush

Paint Colors:

Berry Wine

Butter Pecan

Green Forest

Heartland Blue

Licorice

Maple Syrup

Midnight

Rose Garden

Sunflower

Wicker White

Yellow Ochre

Country Birdhouses

surface: hallway wall

Antique framed collectibles were the focal point of this wall, but I felt it needed some bright colors. I picked up the red, white and blue theme from the adjacent family room, and had some fun with these birdhouses. The variety of detail distinguished each birdhouse, including Americana themes such as stars and stripes. Adding little vines, leaves and mossing warmed the poles and made them less stark, and the bottoms look solidly planted. I felt that the tall, open space needed one very tall birdhouse between the pictures. The exaggerated height added a humorous touch.

The old, rusty-looking watering can needed some ivy painted on it and red geraniums to brighten it up and tie it into the color scheme.

Bluebirds and Nest

I like to make niches or other unexpected places more interesting by adding a trailing vine or tree branch. This is the corner of a wall over a stairwell. I painted a nest with eggs and bluebirds flying to it. To give it a more adult feel, the birds can be painted more realistically, not so cute.

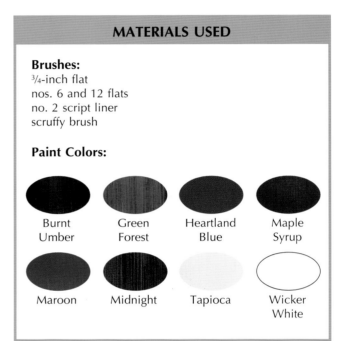

MATERIALS USED

Brushes:
¾-inch flat
nos. 6 and 12 flats
no. 2 script liner
scruffy brush

Paint Colors:

Burnt Umber

Green Forest

Heartland Blue

Maple Syrup

Maroon

Midnight

Tapioca

Wicker White

STAIRS AND HALLWAYS

Lighthouse Cove Mural

surface: staircase wall

Sometimes the odd angles of a short staircase wall can present not only a challenge, but also an opportunity to design a mural that fits into the space in a natural-looking way. Such was the case here. There were only six steps up to a landing, then a sharp right turn that led up the rest of the steps. The angled baseboard brought the wall to a point at the bottom of the steps. The idea of a cove or inlet appealed to me, and I felt I could easily make it fit into the point.

Before I began painting, I studied many pictures of coves, shorelines, lighthouses, water and the kinds of plants found along shores and beaches. While the scene to the right is somewhat fanciful with its three lighthouses, I wanted to make the lighthouses and land masses fairly realistic.

Painting lighthouses is fun—the patterns on real lighthouses are so varied that you can paint almost any design and still have them look realistic. There are books full of colorful photos of lighthouses and their coastal surroundings, so finding a pattern and color scheme you like should be easy.

This is an ideal mural to paint for a man. It can be personalized with sailboats, fishing gear or other details meaningful to him, and the shape of the water can be adapted to look like his favorite shoreline scene.

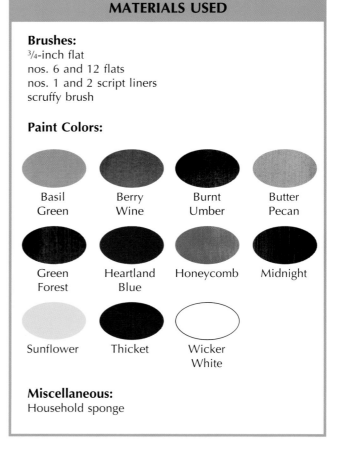

MATERIALS USED

Brushes:
3/4-inch flat
nos. 6 and 12 flats
nos. 1 and 2 script liners
scruffy brush

Paint Colors:

Basil Green · Berry Wine · Burnt Umber · Butter Pecan

Green Forest · Heartland Blue · Honeycomb · Midnight

Sunflower · Thicket · Wicker White

Miscellaneous:
Household sponge

1. Basecoating in the Largest Shapes

First I found a horizon line and started my design from that point. I wanted the viewer to feel as if he were standing on a rocky bluff over-looking an inlet. I sketched the light-houses and land masses with a pen-cil. Then using my dampened sponge, I basecoated in each color. For the water, I used watered-down Heartland Blue, letting some of the white of the wall show through. The foreground rock formations were shaded along their edges to give them form.

2. Adding Details to the Water and Shoreline

Using my sponge side-loaded with Wicker White, I painted in some bil-lowy clouds, foam where the water meets the shore, and streaks of re-flected light in the water. Then with Burnt Umber in the sponge, I shad-owed in more rock formations. I used Basil Green and Butter Pecan to paint in some land masses, and darker Thicket with a scruffy brush to add greenery under the middle lighthouse. Following photos of real lighthouses, I completed the red-striped lighthouse using my no. 6 and no. 12 flat brushes, and sponged in its reflection with a watered-down wash of the same colors.

3. Adding Waves to the Water

Again I side-loaded my sponge with Wicker White and streaked some foamy waves in the water. Using a sponge instead of a brush is much quicker and easier, and gives a softer, more realistic look to the waves.

4. Painting in the Grasses

To add grasses to the foreground, I used the chisel edge of a ¾-inch flat brush double-loaded with Burnt Umber and Wicker White. I also enlarged the rocks and grasses to create the illusion of being closer to the viewer.

5. Adding Sea Oats

For the sea oats, I used Burnt Umber and Wicker White double-loaded on my flat brush with a back-and-forth motion, giving both highlights and shading to the oats.

6. Adding Sunset Colors to the Sky

With a damp sponge lightly loaded with Midnight, I added darker blues to the sky, then streaks of Wicker White for clouds. The setting sun was brushed in with Sunflower.

The lighthouse on the left was based in with Butter Pecan. Blue striping was painted over that, then partially wiped off to create a rounded effect. The door and window were painted in Berry Wine. I added more grasses and sea oats to the base of the lighthouse, building them up so the lighthouse appeared solidly grounded.

7. Finish

I finished the scene by painting Green Forest stripes on the closest lighthouse, with Berry Wine detailing on the roof and doors. I added grasses with a sponge and Basil Green, wrapping the grass around the base.

The setting sun's reflection on the water, pink streaks in the sky and sailboats finished the scene.

chapter 4

walls

surface: textured plaster wall

Decorative painting on walls can be as simple or elaborate as you wish. If wall space is at a premium in your home, a single trailing ivy vine or small garland of flowers may be just enough, or try a floral border around a picture frame or mirror. But if you have a large expanse of wall or an entire roomful of walls to work with, then you have the opportunity to paint a design on a grand scale, like the dining room to the right.

The room's three walls were the original beige textured plaster, which did nothing to set off the richly colored server and plate hutch. I designed a faux-column and grapevine motif that picked up the colors of the hutch and dinnerware, and tied all three walls together with a faux column in each corner. The grapevines give an old-world look, which works well with traditional, country or Mediterranean decors.

To refinish the server and hutch, I lightly steel-wooled the original finish to rough it up so the paint would adhere better, then primed the pieces with a one-coat primer for latex paint. The base coat was two coats of Berry Wine acrylic paint.

On a large, car wash-type sponge, I loaded Alizarin Crimson (FolkArt Artist Pigments) and Berry Wine (the basecoat color) at the same time and pounced the sponge onto the pieces, heavily in some places and lightly in others to create a rich texture. Then, with a ¾-inch flat brush loaded with Alizarin Crimson, I painted the trim moldings on both pieces. Some silk grape leaves and faux grape clusters in antiqued plaster wall planters completed the effect.

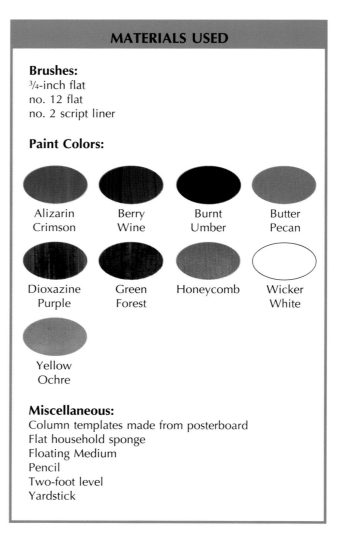

MATERIALS USED

Brushes:
¾-inch flat
no. 12 flat
no. 2 script liner

Paint Colors:

Alizarin Crimson

Berry Wine

Burnt Umber

Butter Pecan

Dioxazine Purple

Green Forest

Honeycomb

Wicker White

Yellow Ochre

Miscellaneous:
Column templates made from posterboard
Flat household sponge
Floating Medium
Pencil
Two-foot level
Yardstick

Faux Columns and Grapevine

surface: textured plaster wall

1. Make a template for the column top out of posterboard or a file folder, and draw one half of the column outline. Then decide how wide you want your column to be. Fold the template in half to equal half of the final width and cut it out. When unfolded, you will have the full column pattern. Repeat this for the base of the column.

Hold the template at the top of the wall under the crown molding. (If the ceiling isn't level, the template won't be either. Use the two-foot level to check your ceiling.) With a pencil, lightly draw around your pattern.

I'm using a fairly simple Ionic design here. For more column design ideas, see the sketches on page 43.

2. Using the level, make certain that the vertical lines of the column are straight. Using a pencil, make hash marks along the level.

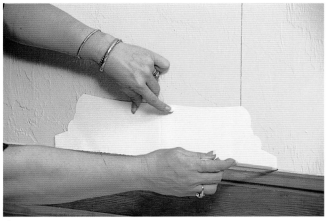

3. Use a yardstick to draw the column lines.

4. Finally, trace around the base of the column pattern to fit.

5. Side load a ¾-inch flat brush with Honeycomb. I used a plain white styrofoam plate as my palette—it's lightweight and easy to hold for a long period of time.

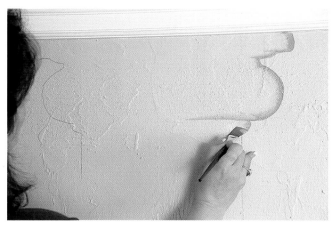

6. Using your side-loaded brush, stroke along the penciled outline, keeping the loaded half of your brush to the outside.

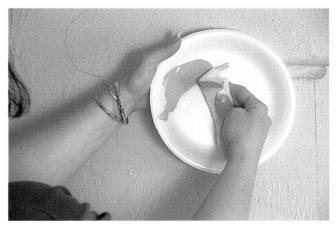

7. Side load a dampened flat household sponge with Honeycomb. To side load a flat sponge, brush one edge of your sponge into your paint, just like side-loading a brush.

8. Keeping the loaded side of the sponge to the outside, stroke down the length of the column until the sponge runs out of paint. Reload with paint (redampening the sponge, if needed) and rub up into the area already painted, then continue downward.

9. To prevent leaving a hard edge, pull the paint toward the center of the column with a circular motion of the sponge.

10. Use a yardstick to pencil in the fluted lines. Double-load a ¾-inch flat brush with Honeycomb and stroke in the curves of the flutes.

11. Again, use the sponge to continue down the flute, keeping the loaded side of the sponge on the correct side for shading. (On the right side of the column, the shading is on the right, and vice versa.) In the center flute, shade both sides to create the illusion of a rounded form.

12. Go back to the column top and, with your side-loaded ¾-inch flat brush, finish the curving details of the design.

13. Work Floating Medium into a clean brush that's been side-loaded with Burnt Umber, and shadow the column to add more depth.

14. Here's what a column looks like on an inverted corner. I used the sponge to paint the fluting.

15. You can also use a ¾-inch sideloaded brush to add more detail, if needed.

16. Here is the completed column on an inverted (inside) corner. You can stop here if you wish, or add whatever details will work in your room. On the next few pages, I'll show you how to add a grapevine that twines up and around the column.

WALLS

17. Double-load your ¾-inch flat brush to fill the bristles at least two-thirds of the way up with Wicker White and Burnt Umber.

18. Using the chisel edge of the brush and leading with the Wicker White, paint vines from behind the column and up to make it appear as though the vine is winding around the column.

19. Stop painting, lift the brush off the wall and move your hand in the direction that the vine would grow behind the column.

20. Then touch the brush down again at the edge of the column where the vine would reappear.

21. Paint the vine across the front of the column again, still working upward.

22. Add more vining to complete the vine on the column and the ceiling.

23. Paint grape leaves and one-stroke leaves with Green Forest and Wicker White double-loaded onto your ¾-inch flat brush. Alternate picking up Burnt Umber and Butter Pecan on one corner of your brush to vary the natural shading of the leaves. Always load the darker shades, such as Burnt Umber, onto the darker side of the brush (here, Green Forest) and the lighter shades, such as Butter Pecan, onto the lighter side of the brush.

24. Paint half of the leaf following the shape of a grape leaf. The dark green edge of your brush is like a pencil drawing the outside edge of the leaf. Then paint the second half in the same manner to complete the leaf, keeping the green edge on the outside.

25. Add new-growth vines occasionally with Green Forest and Wicker White.

26. Begin painting clusters of grapes starting with a no. 12 flat brush double-loaded with Dioxazine Purple and Butter Pecan. To form a grape, paint it in two halves. Starting on the chisel edge, turn the purple corner of the brush in a half circle.

27. To paint the other half, start on the original spot and turn the purple corner of the brush in the opposite direction. Stroke in semi-circular motions to smooth out the grape. Continue painting grapes to form tapering clusters.

28. Add curlicue vines with a no. 2 script liner and inky green paint. To freehand the curlicues, stay on the tip of the brush, bracing your little finger against the wall.

Here are some more column design ideas. Many more examples can be found in books or magazines on colonial architecture.

WALLS

Trailing Ivy

surface: painted wall

Here's a quick and easy way to dress up a man's den or office space: a simple trailing ivy vine. It's a great way to add colorful foliage to a room without getting too flowery and, in this project, the vine ties the fishing objects and old wooden dry sink together.

The trick is to make the vine look natural, which means no straight lines or perfect right angles. Below is an example of an unnatural-looking vine.

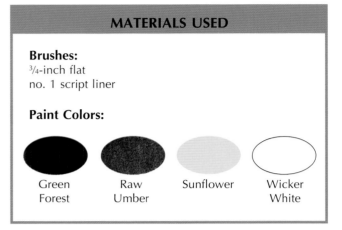

MATERIALS USED

Brushes:
¾-inch flat
no. 1 script liner

Paint Colors:

Green Forest   Raw Umber   Sunflower   Wicker White

Wrong
These vines don't look natural because they're painted straight out like sticks, perpendicular to the doorjamb, and they're the same length.

1. Right

Here I've taken those unnatural sticks and softened them into a more relaxed-looking vine. The vine now looks as if it were growing from the outside in, through the doorjamb, and onto the wall. I used a ¾-inch flat brush double-loaded with Raw Umber and Wicker White, and painted all of the bare vines on the wall first for placement.

2. Adding Leaves

I then painted in my desired leaves with a ¾-inch flat brush double-loaded with Green Forest and Sunflower, picking up Raw Umber occasionally. Placement is important. Be sure that the leaves are not too close together or all pointing in the same direction, and leave some room between the vine and leaves for the connecting stems.

3. Finish

The finished ivy vine looks light and airy because I didn't overdo it. Look carefully at the relationship of the leaves to the vine. The leaves are painted in the direction that the vine is growing, not perpendicular to the vine, and they're attached to stems, not sitting directly on the vine.

To add a humorous touch, I painted a dragonfly in front of the fish plaque.

WALLS

Fast and Easy Faux Finish

surface: textured wall

Applying a faux finish to a painted wall does not need to be a big, expensive production. You can add rich texture to a plain wall with a few colors of acrylic paint and some large sponges. Like everything, though, there's an easy and a hard way to do it. Let me show you how to add a subtly mottled texture to a wall in just a few minutes.

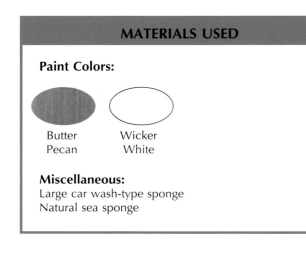

MATERIALS USED

Paint Colors:

Butter Pecan   Wicker White

Miscellaneous:
Large car wash-type sponge
Natural sea sponge

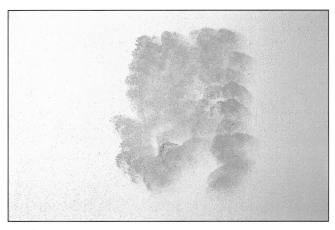

Hard Way—Step 1
Here's an example of the hard way to apply texture to a painted wall. First, I sponged on only my darker color (Butter Pecan) and let it dry.

Hard Way—Step 2
Then I loaded my sponge with only my lighter color (Wicker White) and sponged it over the Butter Pecan. As you can see, the two colors are not blending well and the edges are hard. Not a pretty sight!

Easy Way—Step 1

Now I'll show you how to fix this. Just load *both* colors on your sponge at the same time. Here I've loaded Butter Pecan on the left and Wicker White on the right of my large sponge.

Easy Way—Step 2

Press the double-loaded sponge lightly on the wall, turning and shifting the sponge with each press. Keep working the sponge over the area until all of the hard edges disappear. Do you see the difference? The texture looks so much more natural with many shades from white to tan.

Natural Sea Sponge

This shows another finish, this time using a natural sea sponge loaded half and half with the same two colors. This technique can be used with three or four colors as long as two colors are on the same sponge at the same time.

WALLS

Ficus Tree in an Urn

surface: textured wall

I love painting ficus trees in urns—they work with many different decors. They can be painted where you can't hang a picture because of space, such as a hallway. They're quick and easy to paint, but make a big statement.

You can adapt this idea to different rooms by adding flowers, fruit or ribbons to your trees. Here, I added some subtle "shadow leaves" with Floating Medium and Butter Pecan worked into a no. 12 flat brush. They make the tree look fuller, giving it dimension.

Before I painted the tree and urn on the wall, I added a fast and easy faux finish to the area that would be behind the tree. See pages 46-47 for step-by-step instructions.

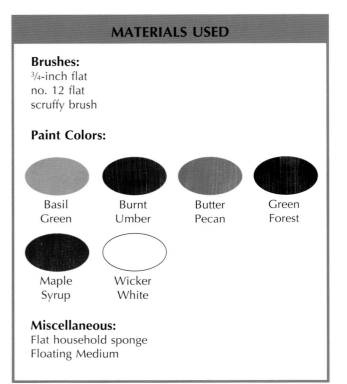

MATERIALS USED

Brushes:
¾-inch flat
no. 12 flat
scruffy brush

Paint Colors:

Basil Green

Burnt Umber

Butter Pecan

Green Forest

Maple Syrup

Wicker White

Miscellaneous:
Flat household sponge
Floating Medium

1. First, draw an urn shape on the wall above the baseboard. I free-handed this one, but you can make your own design on a cardboard template. See page 53 for some urn design ideas, or look through gardening magazines and books.

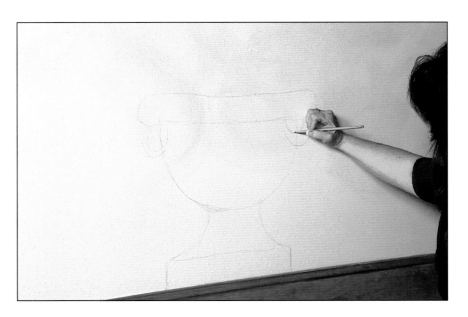

WALLS

2. Dampen a clean, flat household sponge with water, side-load it with Butter Pecan and shade along the outside edge of the urn. Be sure to keep the paint side of the sponge to the outside. Make circular motions with the sponge, pulling a little paint into the center of the urn.

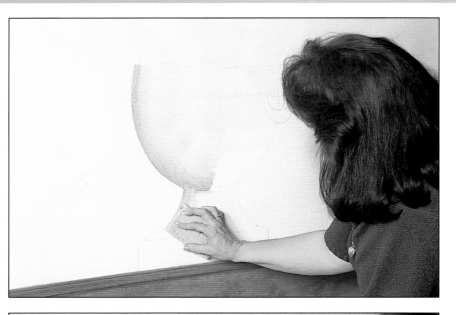

3. Shade the urn's base with a ¾-inch flat brush to create depth. Then with the side-loaded sponge, add roundness to the bottom of the urn body.

4. Again, using the flat sponge, stroke on the big rim at the top of the urn and add the handles with a brush. I used a scruffy brush multi-loaded with Wicker White, Green Forest and Butter Pecan to pounce on moss as if it were hanging over the edge of the urn. I used the edge of the scruffy brush to taper the moss to a point. You can also use a natural sea sponge to add moss if you want a more subtle look.

5. With a ¾-inch flat brush side-loaded with Butter Pecan, add a rose-and-leaves design sculpted onto the side of the urn.

6. Now load your flat brush with Floating Medium and Burnt Umber, and shade along one outside edge of the urn to create a three-dimensional effect.

7. Do the same along one side of the mossy areas. Be sure your shading is always on the same side. It gives the appearance of shadowing, which helps the whole design look three-dimensional.

WALLS

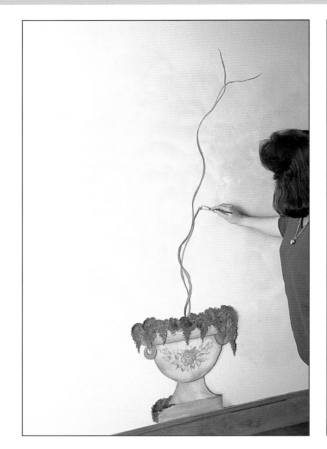

8. (Above) Start painting the trunk of the ficus tree from the base, following the direction of growth. Multiload a ¾-inch flat brush with Burnt Umber, Maple Syrup, Wicker White and a touch of Basil Green. In this photo, you can see the area of the wall where I sponged on a mottled faux finish, which added more depth to the tree. For more interest, I made this ficus tree with a twisting, winding trunk. It may not be botanically accurate, but I like the effect.

9. (Above right) As you draw your brush upward, continue each stroke outward to form the branches. Let them taper off naturally at the tip by releasing pressure on your brush.

10. (Right) Add simple one-stroke leaves and new-growth stems by double-loading your ¾-inch flat brush with Basil Green and Green Forest. The stems and leaves should continue in the direction they would grow. Foliage painted perpendicularly to a branch looks unnatural.

I finished this project by adding shadow leaves for a more realistic look (see the photo on page 49).

This design looks especially nice on the wall of a porch or sunroom, where a potted ficus tree would normally be placed.

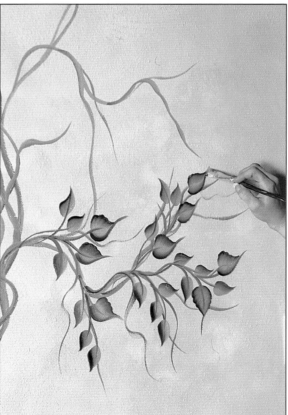

Here are a few more ideas for urn designs. Remember, urns usually rest on a solid base, but I have seen some that can be mounted on walls.

chapter 5

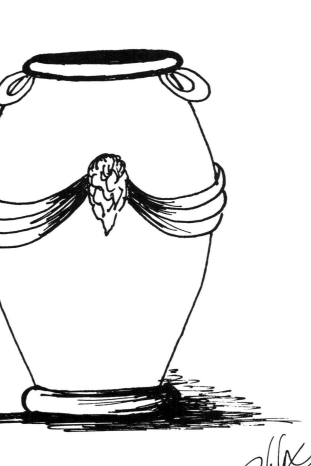

doors and windows

Sunflowers on Window Frame

surface: wood based with satin wall paint

Frames and trim around doors and windows are such a common sight that we may not think about them as places to decorate with paint. But what a great opportunity they give us to add an unexpected personal touch to a room. Even the wall areas above and beside doors and windows can be made more attractive with vining roses or fruit, or even trompe l'oeil door crowns. Just be sure to choose colors that pick up or harmonize with other colors in the room.

The bright yellow sunflowers on the window frame at right are an exciting accent in a room with pale, creamy yellow walls. And the green leaves and vines reflect the foliage of the trees outside the bay window. This design looks great in a guest room or girl's bedroom. It makes a pretty statement in a room that isn't overly furnished or doesn't have any curtains.

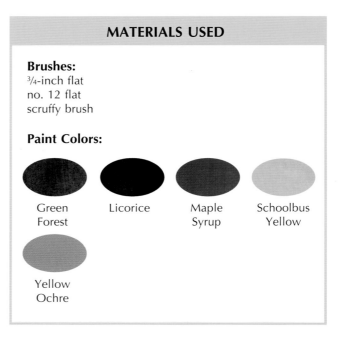

MATERIALS USED

Brushes:
¾-inch flat
no. 12 flat
scruffy brush

Paint Colors:

Green Forest   Licorice   Maple Syrup   Schoolbus Yellow

Yellow Ochre

1. Design Is Too Tight

When dealing with a narrow area like this window frame, you might feel your artwork has to be very small and tight. Actually, in many cases, a more expansive design works better. I would wipe this off with a clean wet rag and start again.

2. Better

Notice the difference when the leaves and vines are open and airy. After painting the vines, I placed my leaves to allow room for the sunflowers.

3. Adding Sunflowers

I painted my large, full sunflowers in the center of the design, then worked outward with smaller buds. To paint the sunflowers, double-load a scruffy brush with Maple Syrup and Licorice and pounce on the dark centers. Then double-load a no. 12 flat brush with Schoolbus Yellow and Yellow Ochre, and stroke petals from the center outward, picking up some of the dark center color to add shading to the petals. Go back in with the scruffy brush and re-pounce the center to regain the shape. Put a little Yellow Ochre on the scruffy and pounce in a highlight on the center.

The smaller leaves are painted with a no. 12 flat brush double-loaded with Schoolbus Yellow and Green Forest.

You can stop here if this is enough or there are curtains at the sides.

Because of the size of the window frame, I continued the design to the corners and partway down both sides, almost like a swag curtain.

Ivy Vine on Wooden Cornice

surface: stained wood

Wooden window cornices are a great treatment in lieu of curtains, or you can add curtains underneath. I stained this cornice to match the woodwork in the room, and painted a casual variegated ivy vine using Wicker White and Green Forest to provide a contrast with the dark wood. I painted the string ribbon that winds among the vine using Midnight and a script liner.

Some clusters of red berries were scattered along the ivy vine to pick up the red accents in the room. I used a no. 12 flat brush double-loaded with Maroon and a little Wicker White to paint the berries.

When the paint was thoroughly dry, I sealed the entire cornice with a couple coats of water-based satin varnish, making the colors look richer. This was a simple project which added a nice touch to a man's study where curtains were not wanted.

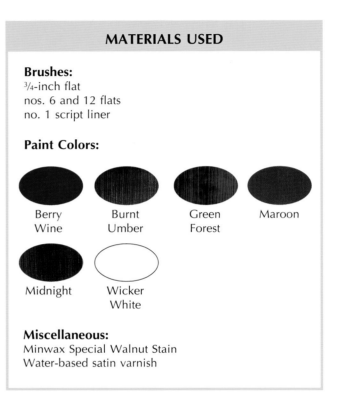

MATERIALS USED

Brushes:
¾-inch flat
nos. 6 and 12 flats
no. 1 script liner

Paint Colors:

Berry Wine   Burnt Umber   Green Forest   Maroon

Midnight   Wicker White

Miscellaneous:
Minwax Special Walnut Stain
Water-based satin varnish

Wisteria and Rosebud Border

surface: textured plaster wall

Often between the top of a door frame and the bottom of the ceiling's crown molding is just enough space to paint a nice-sized border. Choose a design that fits comfortably in that space without looking crowded.

The wisteria and rosebud border shown to the right is a quick and easy painting project for kitchens, girls' bedrooms and bathrooms. You can change the colors or types of flowers to fit your tastes and color schemes. The colors I used here work beautifully on neutral backgrounds.

This border was extended beyond the door frame to the corners of the wall, but you can drape the border down both sides of the door instead. Either way, it's best to start your design above the door frame so you know that it will fit nicely.

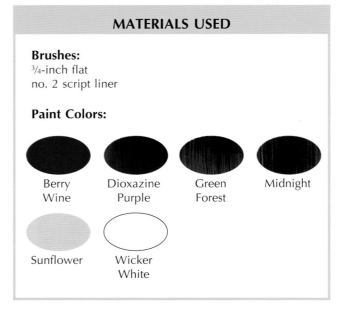

MATERIALS USED

Brushes:
3/4-inch flat
no. 2 script liner

Paint Colors:

Berry Wine   Dioxazine Purple   Green Forest   Midnight

Sunflower   Wicker White

DOORS AND WINDOWS

1. Paint a simple curving vine with a ¾-inch flat brush double-loaded with Green Forest and Wicker White. Make sure the vine is large and loose.

2. Every six inches or so, trail vines off the main vine, always starting on one side of the vine and crossing over. If you're painting on a textured wall like this one, don't be concerned that your lines are breaking up or have rough edges. It just adds to the charm!

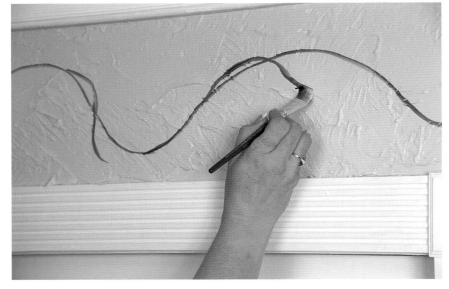

3. Double load a ¾-inch flat brush with Berry Wine and Wicker White, and add small rosebuds. Place the rosebuds at least twelve inches apart. Every so often, I like to put two rosebuds together for variety.

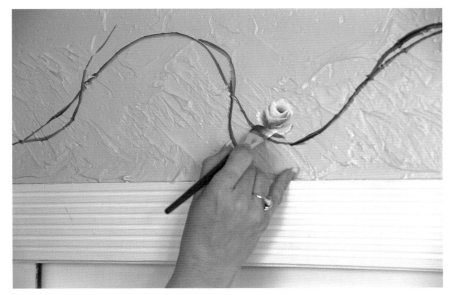

4. Add assorted one-stroke leaves using your vine colors. Remember, paint the leaves *away* from the vine and connect them with stems to create an airy effect.

5. Pounce on wisteria with a big scruffy brush loaded with Dioxazine Purple, Midnight and Wicker White. Always keep Wicker White on one corner edge of the scruffy and alternate Dioxazine Purple and Midnight on the other corner. I placed the wisteria randomly between the roses.

6. Finish with new-growth stems and curlicues to fill in a few empty spaces. Thin some Green Forest with water to an inky consistency and use your script liner.

Cabbage Roses and Ribbons

surface: painted wall

An unusually shaped window can sometimes present a decorating challenge. You don't want to hide it behind curtains, yet it often needs something to help set it off.

This octagonal window was the sole point of interest on an otherwise blank wall in a young girl's bathroom. The little shirts hanging on the wall were the girl's nightshirts as a baby. I decided to pick up the delicate colors of the embroidery with a rose garland painted to enhance the shape of the window and the beautiful view beyond.

The center of the design is a cluster of large cabbage roses, with smaller rosebuds trailing off to both sides. The pink roses were painted with Rose Garden and Wicker White; the yellow roses were created with Yellow Ochre and Wicker White. Both were painted with a double-loaded ¾-inch flat brush. Then, with a no. 12 flat brush double-loaded with Wicker White and Sterling Blue, I painted big loops of blue ribbon in the center of the rose cluster and trailing ribbon curling down the sides of the window.

Finally, I used Wicker White and Thicket to paint the large leaves around the center roses, trailing vines in and out of the ribbon and adding smaller leaves as filler. The garland looks airy and delicate because the vines are loose and open, not tightly packed together.

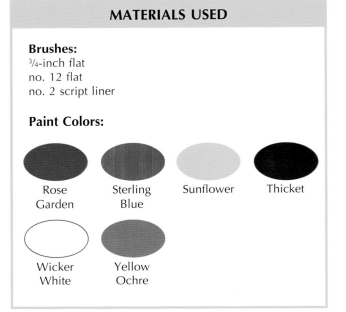

MATERIALS USED

Brushes:
¾-inch flat
no. 12 flat
no. 2 script liner

Paint Colors:

Rose Garden

Sterling Blue

Sunflower

Thicket

Wicker White

Yellow Ochre

Fruit and Grapevine

surface: painted kitchen wall

What better place to paint a fruit and grape-vine motif than in the kitchen? While it's not always feasible to paint above the tops of built-in cabinets, the wall space over a doorway creates a nice focal point when going in and out of the kitchen.

The fruit and vine design shown here could have been centered over the door, but I chose a more interesting wandering effect. The vine appears to grow from behind the door, is heavier in one corner, disappears a little behind the door-jamb, crosses over the corner, and grows down the next wall.

I chose the colors for the fruits from the fabrics and wallpaper in the room. The wall had been painted with a satin interior house paint in a bluish-green that picked up one of the wallpaper colors. Many acrylic paint companies sell a vast array of colors, which makes it easier to match fabrics without having to mix colors. Just take some swatches with you when you buy your paints.

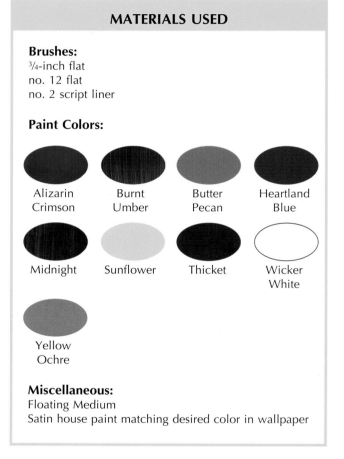

MATERIALS USED

Brushes:
¾-inch flat
no. 12 flat
no. 2 script liner

Paint Colors:

Alizarin Crimson

Burnt Umber

Butter Pecan

Heartland Blue

Midnight

Sunflower

Thicket

Wicker White

Yellow Ochre

Miscellaneous:
Floating Medium
Satin house paint matching desired color in wallpaper

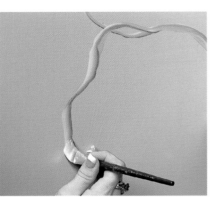

1. To paint the vines, I used a ¾-inch flat brush. First I double-loaded it with Sunflower and Thicket, then I picked up a little Wicker White on the Sunflower corner and a little Heartland Blue on the Thicket corner to multiload the brush. I painted the vines on the chisel edge, leading with the lighter colors.

2. Picking up more of the same colors, I stroked one half of a grape leaf—watching the Thicket edge of my brush for the shape. I then stroked in the second half to complete the leaf, being certain to use the outer edge of the brush like a pencil to draw the shape of the leaf.

3. I pulled stems from the vine into the leaf with the chisel edge of the same brush. On each vine, I painted a few one-stroke leaves with the ¾-inch flat brush, but most were painted with the no. 12 flat.

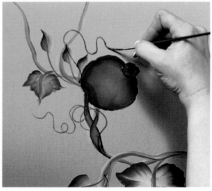

4. Clusters of grapes were painted next. I double-loaded a no.12 flat brush with Heartland Blue and Wicker White, occasionally picking up a little Midnight on the Heartland Blue corner of the brush to add more depth to the shading.

5. Pomegranates are a nice change from red apples. I double-loaded Alizarin Crimson and Sunflower on a ¾-inch flat brush, and painted the pomegranate using the Alizarin Crimson corner of the brush like a pencil to draw the outside edge of the pomegranate.

6. I smoothed out the paint in the center with light strokes, being careful not to overblend, which would muddy the colors. Then with the no. 12 flat double-loaded with Alizarin Crimson and Sunflower, I painted the seed pod on the bottom of the pomegranate. I used the tip of a script liner and Alizarin Crimson to dot seeds in the pod. I also used the script liner and inky Thicket to paint new-growth vines and curlicues.

Complementing Wallpaper

This door is on the wall opposite the one shown on page 67. It leads from a kitchen hallway out to a deck. I continued with the wandering vine here, painting a fruit and vine motif that was more open for this larger wall area. Remember, less is more. You can always add more fruits and leaves if you need to, but removing an overdone painting is difficult and time-consuming.

I chose colors that complemented the wallpaper in the adjacent kitchen nook, and selectively painted some fruit from the wallpaper rather than copying everything in the paper.

DOORS AND WINDOWS

Hydrangeas

surface: painted wall

I love painting hydrangeas. They're easy to paint and fit with many different styles of decor, from contemporary to country to traditional. You can use multiple colors in the blossoms, from soft peaches and pinks to dark blues and burgundies.

The setting at the right is a large window in a master bath. Before painting the flowers around the window, I sponged in shading that complemented the warm tones of the drapery.

Double-loading Butter Pecan and Burnt Umber on a ¾-inch flat brush, I painted curving branches for the hydrangeas. Next, the leaves were painted with Green Forest and Wicker White double-loaded on a ¾-inch flat. Occasionally I picked up Burnt Umber in the leaves rather than white. Hydrangea leaves can be a little larger than other leaves. With a no. 12 flat, I dry-brushed on some one-stroke shadow leaves and used Burnt Umber thinned to an inky consistency to add new-growth curlicues coming off the branches.

To finish, I painted clusters of hydrangeas. For the blue blossoms, I double-loaded a no. 12 flat brush with Wicker White and Midnight; for the pink ones, Wicker White and Berry Wine; and for the mauve, Wicker White and Violet Pansy. If you wish, you can dot in some yellow centers with the end of your brush handle.

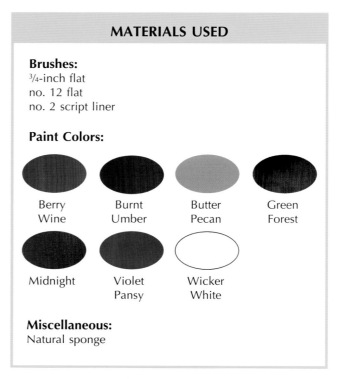

MATERIALS USED

Brushes:
¾-inch flat
no. 12 flat
no. 2 script liner

Paint Colors:

Berry Wine   Burnt Umber   Butter Pecan   Green Forest

Midnight   Violet Pansy   Wicker White

Miscellaneous:
Natural sponge

1

2

3

4

5

living and family rooms

Rose Garland on Wooden Mantel

surface: varnished wood

Most living rooms and family rooms offer a wealth of decorative painting opportunities, including fireplace mantelpieces, bookcases, coffee tables, cathedral ceilings, windows, doors and floors. A well-planned design can tie many elements together within a room as well as unify a room with its neighboring rooms or hallways.

The living room shown to the right was filled with wonderful antiques, family photos and old tapestries. The homeowner wanted something interesting for the large, flat area on the wooden fireplace mantel. We chose a painted design that accented an antique tapestry on the sofa. The largest, darkest rose was centered on the mantel with smaller, lighter roses and buds tapering toward each end. Then I painted vines leading to each flower to give structure to the garland, adding larger leaves in the center and smaller leaves toward the outer ends of the mantelpiece.

Because we wanted a lush look, I painted a lot of little clusters of blue hydrangeas and trailing yellow flowers. New-growth vines and curlicues were added with inky Green Forest and a script liner.

Instead of applying a sealer after the paint was thoroughly dry, I used a soft cloth to rub on Old English Furniture Oil that had a stain in it. This gave an aged look to the painting that matched the patina of the wooden mantelpiece. When it was totally dry, I sprayed on a light coat of flat sealer.

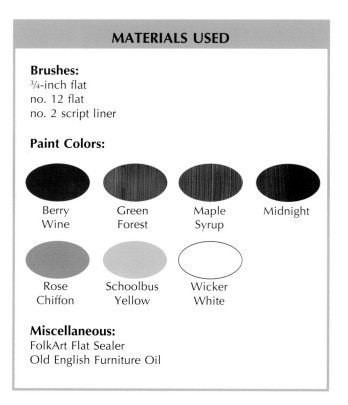

MATERIALS USED

Brushes:
¾-inch flat
no. 12 flat
no. 2 script liner

Paint Colors:

Berry Wine   Green Forest   Maple Syrup   Midnight

Rose Chiffon   Schoolbus Yellow   Wicker White

Miscellaneous:
FolkArt Flat Sealer
Old English Furniture Oil

Rose Garland Over Palladian Window

surface: painted wall

The graceful arch of a Palladian window can be framed with a painted design that picks up other elements in the room. This window is in the same room as the fireplace mantel shown on the previous page. The rose garland was adapted from the flat design on the mantelpiece to fit the curve of the window. It is the middle window in a set of three along the same wall. Since curtains or drapes would have been too much, I put a simple swag at each window, making the painting the focal point.

To soften the contrast between the colorful flowers and the white wall, I first sponged some soft, taupey Butter Pecan on the wall before painting the garland.

I painted in all of the branches with double-loaded Maple Syrup and Wicker White to help lay out my design. The cabbage roses were painted next, with the largest ones in the center of the arch. The darker roses were painted with Berry Wine and Wicker White, and the lighter pink ones with Rose Chiffon and Wicker White.

I added various sizes of one-stroke leaves using Green Forest and Wicker White. Then I filled in with small clusters of blue hydrangeas painted in Midnight and Wicker White double-loaded on my no. 12 flat brush.

Some trailing flowers were painted with Schoolbus Yellow and Wicker White, and I finished with curlicues of inky Green Forest.

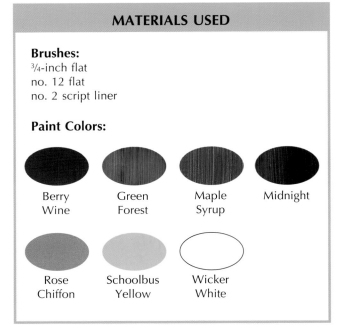

MATERIALS USED

Brushes:
3/4-inch flat
no. 12 flat
no. 2 script liner

Paint Colors:

Berry Wine

Green Forest

Maple Syrup

Midnight

Rose Chiffon

Schoolbus Yellow

Wicker White

LIVING AND FAMILY ROOMS

Blueberries and Vine

surface: painted wooden table

There's nothing like a beautiful piece of hand-painted furniture to start a conversation going, especially when it's a design you've created and painted yourself. If you have an old, beat-up table, chair or chest of drawers you've been thinking of refinishing, why not paint it instead? Sanding, staining and refinishing wood furniture can be a long and tedious process, and if the wood is not of high quality, it's almost not worth the trouble.

Hand-painted furniture is rapidly gaining in popularity, and it's no wonder considering how easy it is to paint with today's acrylic paints. The numerous colors available make it possible to match nearly any decor, and if you don't like your results, it's easy enough to paint over what you've done. Another advantage is that the bare wood need not be presanded to a silken finish. A few nicks and dents add to the charm, and if the wood has deep discolorations or stains, the paint will cover them completely.

The rich red table shown to the right was an old pine table that time (along with kids and dogs) had distressed. With a natural blueberries-and-vine motif around the edge, it made an unfussy addition to a casual family room.

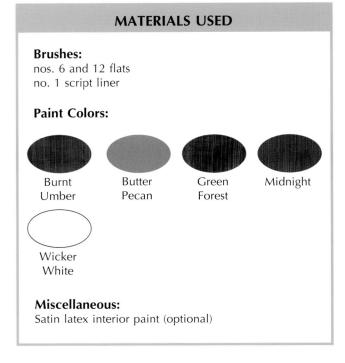

MATERIALS USED

Brushes:
nos. 6 and 12 flats
no. 1 script liner

Paint Colors:

Burnt Umber   Butter Pecan   Green Forest   Midnight

Wicker White

Miscellaneous:
Satin latex interior paint (optional)

1. Beginning With the Vine

After sanding, I basecoated the entire table with a satin latex paint in a color that matched the room decor. With a no. 12 flat brush double-loaded with Burnt Umber and Wicker White, I painted loose, flowing vines around the edge, always leading with the white corner of the brush. Vines are quick and easy to paint if you stay up on the chisel edge of your brush.

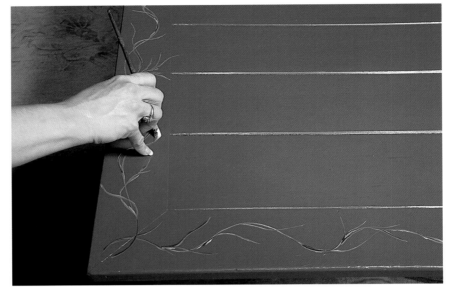

2. Painting One-Stroke Leaves

With Green Forest and Wicker White double-loaded on a no. 6 flat, I painted little clusters of one-stroke leaves around the edge, making sure the majority of leaves were slightly separated from the vine.

3. Adding Stems

With the no. 1 script liner, I mixed Green Forest with water to an inky consistency. I then stroked the brush into Wicker White for highlights and painted little stems leading from the vines into the centers of the leaves.

4. Painting the Blueberries

With a no. 6 flat brush double-loaded with Midnight and Wicker White, I painted the blueberries in a semicircular motion, keeping the Midnight on the outside. Then I dotted Wicker White on the blossom end of some selected berries, and connected the blueberries to the vines with stems painted with a no. 1 script liner and Butter Pecan.

5. Finish

Now it looks like a valuable (and expensive) piece of furniture, yet simple strokework and a few colors were all it took to bring an old table back to life.

Trompe L'Oeil Signs and Wood Shelf

surface: painted wall

When deciding what sort of painted decor would work in a man's den or office, remember to keep it fairly subdued and uncomplicated. I like to add greenery, trees, vines or tropical plants. It's even okay to add berries, but I prefer to stay away from florals. Other themes men appreciate include signs, sports, hunting, the jungle, marine life, lighthouses, the beach, cars, trains and hot air balloons. You can find ideas from postcards, greeting cards, magazines and catalogs.

The game room/den to the right included a pool table, board games, collectibles and fishing and hunting gear. I painted a collection of trompe l'oeil signs around a real wooden sign using rich, dark colors to give a masculine look. Inca Gold highlights and some shadows floated along the sides of the signs create a three-dimensional effect.

To fill in an empty spot among the antiques on the wall opposite the signs, I painted a wooden shelf illusion with a basket of ivy, collection of books, fishing fly and wooden fish. I basecoated all of these items first, then added the details, texture and ivy flowing over the shelf. I floated some shadowing under the shelf for depth.

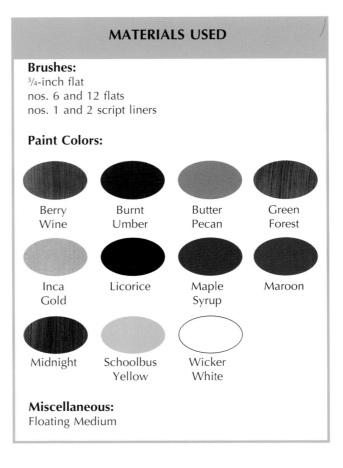

MATERIALS USED

Brushes:
¾-inch flat
nos. 6 and 12 flats
nos. 1 and 2 script liners

Paint Colors:

Berry Wine

Burnt Umber

Butter Pecan

Green Forest

Inca Gold

Licorice

Maple Syrup

Maroon

Midnight

Schoolbus Yellow

Wicker White

Miscellaneous:
Floating Medium

Game Room Signs

Trompe L'Oeil Shelf

Country Stores Fireplace Screen

surface: unpainted plywood

Fireplace screens are so much fun to paint and can add delightful accents to a living room or family room for any season of the year. The country stores shown to the right were personalized with the homeowner's family names, but it is easily adaptable to the hobbies, interests and names of your family members, including your pets. The colors can be changed to match your decor.

I began with 1″×12″ pine boards cut six inches taller than the fireplace opening, cutting out different roof lines for variety. I stained the boards and then hinged them together in an accordion-fold fashion.

Hank's Boats—The roof, chimney and boat were basecoated with Butter Pecan. The windows, doors and sign were basecoated with Maroon. I used Burnt Umber to create the illusion of planks on the stained board. With a scruffy brush, I pounced on foliage at the base of the building, then painted a yellow blossom vine up the chimney.

The Country Store—I basecoated the board with Heartland Blue, the roof with Maroon and the windows and doors with Midnight. I pounced greenery at the base and a wisteria vine up the side of the building. Wicker White on a liner brush was used to detail the signs.

Post Office—This was basecoated with Maroon, the roof and sign with Butter Pecan and the steps and doors with Licorice. I pounced some foliage on the tree with Wicker White and Green Forest, and added a small vine and the flag.

Antiques—The building was basecoated with Sterling Blue, the roof with Maroon (with Burnt Umber shingles) and the windows, doors and sign with Midnight. I used the scruffy brush to pounce on Schoolbus Yellow, Green Forest and Wicker White for flowers in the window boxes. The name was painted using Wicker White and Maroon.

Nikki's Nick Nacks—Olive Green was used to basecoat the building, Burnt Umber for the roof and Maroon for the chimney. I pounced wisteria up the chimney with Dioxazine Purple and Wicker White. The lettering and heart were painted with Violet Pansy, the dalmatian with Wicker White and Burnt Umber and the sign with Tapioca.

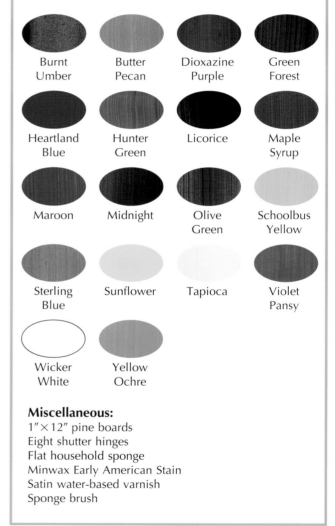

MATERIALS USED

Brushes:
¾-inch flat
nos. 2, 6 and 12 flats
nos. 1 and 2 script liners (for lettering)
small and regular scruffy brushes

Paint Colors:

Burnt Umber | Butter Pecan | Dioxazine Purple | Green Forest

Heartland Blue | Hunter Green | Licorice | Maple Syrup

Maroon | Midnight | Olive Green | Schoolbus Yellow

Sterling Blue | Sunflower | Tapioca | Violet Pansy

Wicker White | Yellow Ochre

Miscellaneous:
1″×12″ pine boards
Eight shutter hinges
Flat household sponge
Minwax Early American Stain
Satin water-based varnish
Sponge brush

Yellow Rose Floorcloth

surface: wood floor

Floorcloths are a popular decorating item these days, but for the little area rug shown to the right, I chose to take the term "floorcloth" literally. I painted it directly on the floor. It was located in a casual family room in front of French doors leading out to a porch. The floor's pine boards and uneven nailing were a bit rustic looking but, rather than trying to cover them up with paint, I let them show through. The floor had already been stained, then finished with polyurethane.

The shading and the fringe on both sides give a realistic, trompe l'oeil effect, and the advantage of a painted floorcloth is that it never gets rumpled or dirty!

For this area, the size of the French doors determined the size of the floorcloth. Or you could just use the measurements of an existing rug in your home that you like.

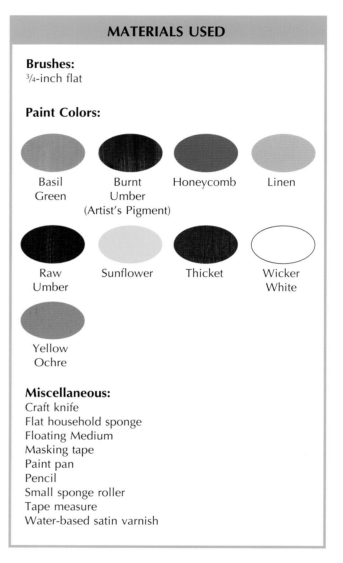

MATERIALS USED

Brushes:
¾-inch flat

Paint Colors:

Basil Green

Burnt Umber (Artist's Pigment)

Honeycomb

Linen

Raw Umber

Sunflower

Thicket

Wicker White

Yellow Ochre

Miscellaneous:
Craft knife
Flat household sponge
Floating Medium
Masking tape
Paint pan
Pencil
Small sponge roller
Tape measure
Water-based satin varnish

1. Measuring and Taping

To decide how wide to make the outer band, first determine how much of the design you want to include in the middle. Your taping job will make a big difference in producing a clean, finished look, so measure and mark carefully. (The taping may take longer than the actual painting!)

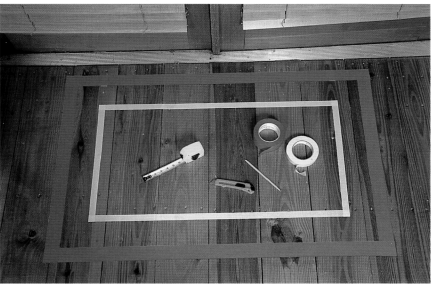

2. Basecoating the Center

I used a sponge roller loaded with Honeycomb to basecoat the center portion first because it's always easier to start in the middle and work outward. After it dried, I rolled on a second coat.

3. Basecoating the Outer Band

I rolled two coats of Linen on the outer band and didn't wait for the center to dry. You will get a nicer edge if you remove the tape while the paint's still a little wet.

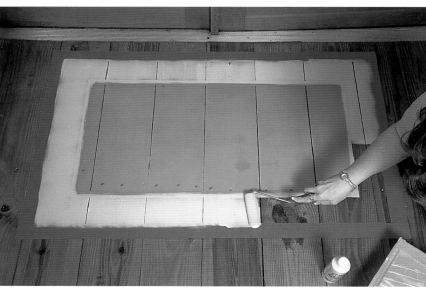

4. Adding the Shading

To complement the aged character of the wood floor, I shaded the basecoat using Burnt Umber and a flat household sponge. With a circular motion, gradually work the shading inward.

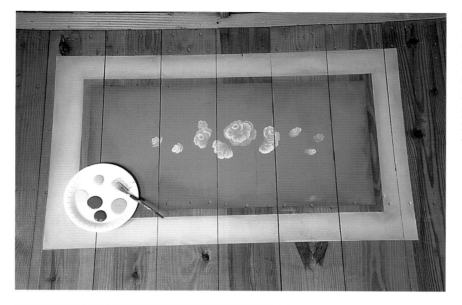

5. Painting the Center Roses

I chose a floral design to complement the room decor. The yellow cabbage roses were painted with Yellow Ochre and Wicker White double-loaded on a ¾-inch flat brush. I painted the large roses in the center first and worked my way outward with smaller ones.

6. Adding Leaves and Stems

To fill in foliage around and between the roses, I double-loaded a ¾-inch flat brush with Sunflower and Thicket, occasionally picking up Basil Green, and stroked on the larger leaves. The smaller leaves used the same colors, but I switched to a no. 12 flat brush.

Then I worked Raw Umber and Floating Medium into my brush to paint some shadow leaves. They're silhouetted around the spray of flowers.

7. Finish

To connect the center portion of the rug to the outer band, I painted criss-crosses freehand using a no. 12 flat brush double-loaded with Burnt Umber and Honeycomb. Then I double-loaded a ¾-inch flat with Wicker White and Burnt Umber and, staying up on the chisel edge of the brush, painted fringe at both ends of the rug. After it was dry, I rolled on two to three coats of a water-based satin varnish to protect it from wear.

Topiary Fireplace Screen

surface: unfinished pine

This fireplace screen was one of my first painting projects, yet I still love it because of its simplicity and the good memories it brings.

I had unfinished pine boards cut to shape, then sanded the edges smooth. Before hinging the boards together accordion-style, I mixed a creamy, off-white acrylic paint (Tapioca) with water to make a light wash, applied it with a sponge and let it dry.

I painted the planters and trunks first with Butter Pecan and Maple Syrup. Then I sponged in the topiary balls with a damp sponge loaded with Thicket and Wicker White. Loading the scruffy brush with the same colors, I pounced moss inside the planters.

With a no. 12 flat brush double-loaded with Midnight and Wicker White, I painted the ribbons under the topiary balls, then added Berry Wine and Wicker White ribbons. With Thicket and Wicker White, I painted one-stroke leaves in the ball of each topiary and green vines and one-stroke leaves on the planters. I added little rosebuds in the topiary with Berry Wine.

Along the outer edges of the screen, I painted vines with Wicker White and Thicket, occasionally picking up Green Forest. Then I finished with ribbons woven among the vines, using the same colors as the ribbons under the topiaries.

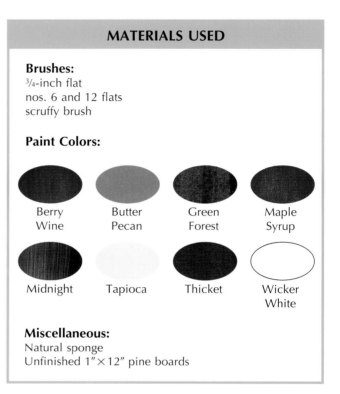

MATERIALS USED

Brushes:
¾-inch flat
nos. 6 and 12 flats
scruffy brush

Paint Colors:

Berry Wine   Butter Pecan   Green Forest   Maple Syrup

Midnight   Tapioca   Thicket   Wicker White

Miscellaneous:
Natural sponge
Unfinished 1″×12″ pine boards

kitchens and dining rooms

Apples and Vine Border

surface: painted wall

The kitchen is the busiest room in many homes and should be a place where you can enjoy all the time you spend there. What better way to enjoy it than to decorate it with a design you love? While kitchens usually have limited surfaces on which to paint, many are adjacent to some sort of dining alcove or breakfast nook. A design that can be carried through both areas looks great and helps unify the two spaces.

It's important to choose a design and colors that are appropriate to the style and age of the kitchen. A sleek, contemporary kitchen with stainless steel appliances might look a little odd with pastel flowers or whimsical country folk painted on the walls. But an old-fashioned, farmhouse kitchen might look fine with both.

The large, open kitchen to the right had traditional cabinetry and warm wooden counters, and the homeowner wanted to use fruit as the main theme. I painted a green vining border with red apples, yellow pears, orange pomegranates, purple grapes and blue plums, which picked up the bright primary colors of the adjoining family room. We mingled the fruit border with antiques on top of the cabinets and added a fruit garland beneath the clock.

The deep corner over the built-in oven presented a problem. I couldn't reach the walls to paint the border! So we disguised the empty corner with large, antique jugs and wound real grapevines and berries around the jugs. This gave more dimension to the border.

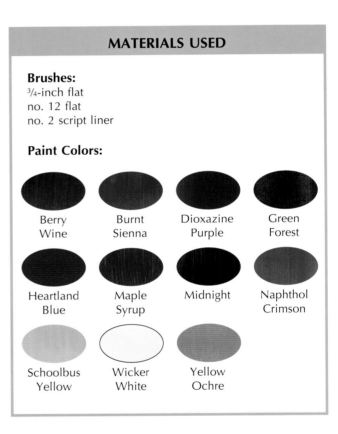

MATERIALS USED

Brushes:
¾-inch flat
no. 12 flat
no. 2 script liner

Paint Colors:

Berry Wine	Burnt Sienna	Dioxazine Purple	Green Forest
Heartland Blue	Maple Syrup	Midnight	Naphthol Crimson
Schoolbus Yellow	Wicker White	Yellow Ochre	

Watermelon and Fruit

surface: painted wall

Dining rooms and breakfast nooks may offer more space for decorative painting than kitchens since there's usually a window to work around or an available blank wall.

This little dining alcove adjoined the kitchen shown on the previous page, but had predictable white walls and sliding glass doors. To tie the rooms together, I continued the fruit and vine border with the same bright colors. But for a touch of whimsy, I painted a bright red watermelon slice as the center of interest over the doors.

The watermelon was painted first, then the vines were added following the shape of the drapes. I added apples, plums, pears, pomegranates and grapes, clustering some of them in twos along the vine. Finally, some one-stroke leaves, fruit blossoms and a few cherries filled out the design.

The material for the drapes and tablecloth was chosen to pick up the reds and blues in the rooms and to echo the fruit theme. The reverse of the drapes is the same bright red as the watermelon. A tray of fruit on the table completes the look.

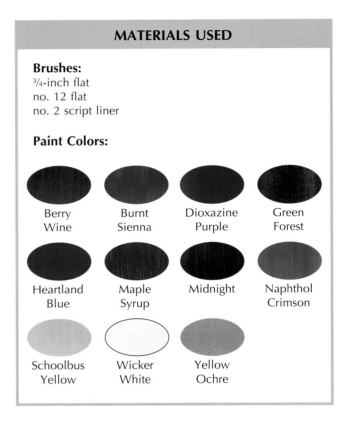

MATERIALS USED

Brushes:
3/4-inch flat
no. 12 flat
no. 2 script liner

Paint Colors:

Berry Wine

Burnt Sienna

Dioxazine Purple

Green Forest

Heartland Blue

Maple Syrup

Midnight

Naphthol Crimson

Schoolbus Yellow

Wicker White

Yellow Ochre

Berries and Vines

surface: textured wall

If your eat-in kitchen or dining alcove has a beautiful view like this one, which overlooks a lake, you wouldn't want to paint a distracting design or one that takes center stage. In this case, the homeowner wanted something simple for the blank wall between the window frame and the corner. Space was too limited for a real potted plant, so I decided to paint one.

The textured plaster wall had been faux finished for an old-world effect. The wall's original color was a warm light tan. A subtle antique look was added by loading a large sponge with a darker tan or taupe shade and rubbing it in a circular motion over the textured wall. The texture picked up and held the color.

The textured wall also gave the painted urn its own texture, so it took just a little shading and some moss to make the urn look old. I painted the large main vine first to help lay out the design as it moved up the wall and over the corner of the window. Then I painted the leaves, not overdoing the large leaves, and filled in with little one-stroke leaves, which gave a lighter, airier effect. I painted in some new-growth vines and curlicues with the vine color and finished with berries to match the color of the adjoining wall.

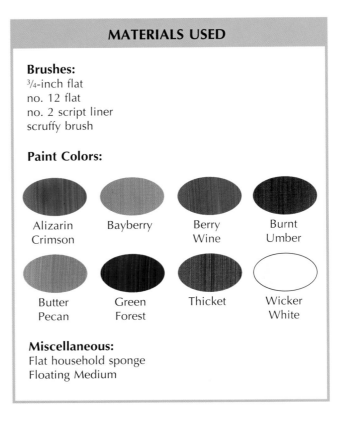

MATERIALS USED

Brushes:
3/4-inch flat
no. 12 flat
no. 2 script liner
scruffy brush

Paint Colors:

Alizarin Crimson

Bayberry

Berry Wine

Burnt Umber

Butter Pecan

Green Forest

Thicket

Wicker White

Miscellaneous:
Flat household sponge
Floating Medium

Arching Grapevine

surface: textured wall

This kitchen was very large and open with a dining alcove and an adjacent, high-ceilinged family room. Rather than painting a single border around the entire space, I felt it would be more tasteful to decorate a few featured areas.

This picturesque Palladian window over the kitchen sink provided a spectacular view, so to eliminate the need for curtains, I decided to drape grapevines over the arch and down almost to the counters. The size of the window allowed a larger, more complex design, which didn't overwhelm the view.

When painting a grapevine like this, I like the branches to look heavy, gnarled and asymmetric, just as they would in nature. Some vines are heavier and branch out more, while others are less so. The lower trailing ends are just about equidistant from the countertop, but the vines and fruits along the sides should not be a mirror image of each other.

As always, I started by placing the vines first to create the layout. I painted a cluster of grapes at the top, then spaced more clusters down each side, leaving room for the plums and cherries. For fun, I added a bluebird flying to its nest, then finished with large and small leaves and curlicues.

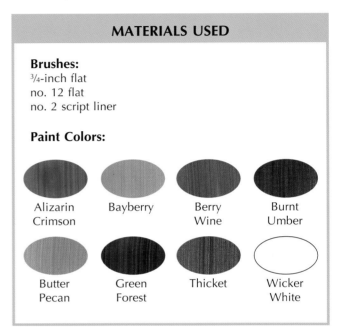

MATERIALS USED

Brushes:
¾-inch flat
no. 12 flat
no. 2 script liner

Paint Colors:

Alizarin Crimson | Bayberry | Berry Wine | Burnt Umber

Butter Pecan | Green Forest | Thicket | Wicker White

Grapevine Over Stove Alcove

surface: textured wall

In the same kitchen as shown on the previous page is this intriguingly shaped alcove for the cooktop. It's located opposite the Palladian window and has the same textured and faux-finished wall surface. I decided that a smaller version of the arching grapevine used over the window would work well here, but I didn't copy it exactly.

Instead of grape clusters, I centered two plums, then trailed off to the sides with grapes and a few cherries. I wanted the most interesting part to be the vining itself and how it follows the gentle curve of the arch. I didn't want the fruits and leaves to overpower the interest of the vine, so this was a more open and airy version of the design painted over the window. The painting procedure and colors were the same. I floated some shadowing around some of the fruit and vines to create the illusion of a three-dimensional spray hanging on the wall.

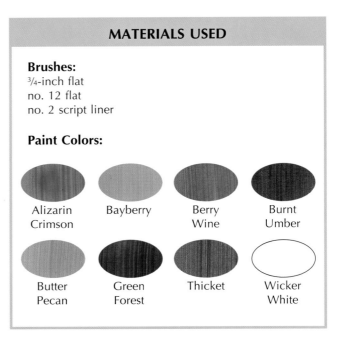

MATERIALS USED

Brushes:
¾-inch flat
no. 12 flat
no. 2 script liner

Paint Colors:

Alizarin Crimson

Bayberry

Berry Wine

Burnt Umber

Butter Pecan

Green Forest

Thicket

Wicker White

Old-World Fruit Table

surface: wood

Have you even seen a great old table at an auction or yard sale but felt it was too far gone to save? The table in my own dining room (shown to the right) should help change your mind about what can be done with old furniture. In its original condition, I was convinced this table was not salvageable. I was going to throw it away, but then decided to experiment with some faux finishes as a last-ditch effort before giving up on it. Besides, with seven children, I needed a large table that could withstand holiday gatherings as well as day-to-day use.

I wanted the table to have an old-world look, with the rich depth and shading of an antique finish. The easiest way to attain that was to use a crackling medium. To prepare the table, I lightly steel-wooled the top to remove any surface dirt. Then, with a household latex satin-finish paint mixed to match the Berry Wine color used on the plate hutch, I basecoated the tabletop using a small foam roller to prevent brush marks. Two coats were necessary for complete coverage.

When the base coat was dry, I rolled on Crackle Medium with another sponge roller and let it dry for at least an hour. I brushed on my chosen color of acrylic paint (Barn Wood) with a house-painting brush and it immediately began to crackle. Once the whole tabletop was crackled, I let it dry completely. (If you would like to see how to use a crackling medium, turn to pages 104-105 for a quick step-by-step demonstration.)

Now the table was ready to be painted with the fruit and grapevine design I had chosen to match the grapevines on my dining room walls. The next page shows a close-up detail of the finished tabletop with the fruit and grapevine design painted on and the final antiquing done.

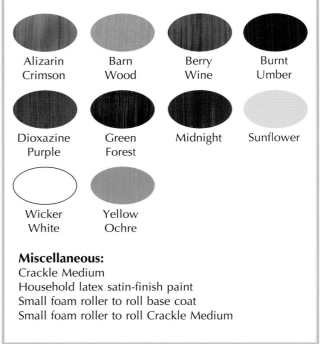

MATERIALS USED

Brushes:
¾-inch flat
no. 12 flat
no. 2 script liner
Three small house-painting brushes

Paint Colors:

Alizarin Crimson

Barn Wood

Berry Wine

Burnt Umber

Dioxazine Purple

Green Forest

Midnight

Sunflower

Wicker White

Yellow Ochre

Miscellaneous:
Crackle Medium
Household latex satin-finish paint
Small foam roller to roll base coat
Small foam roller to roll Crackle Medium

Detail of Old-World Fruit Table

surface: wood

Here is a bird's-eye view of half of the long dining room table shown on the previous page. You can see little areas of the Berry Wine-colored base coat showing through and how the crackling seems to follow the grain of the wood.

To begin the fruit and grapevine design, I painted the main vine around the edge of the table for placement, keeping it open and airy, with a ¾-inch flat double-loaded with Burnt Umber and Wicker White. Then I began adding the fruits one at a time around the table, watching my placement. I painted all of the pears at one time, then all of the apples, all of the cherries and so on, choosing colors already in my decor. You can easily adapt this design to your own color scheme. After I finished the fruits, I added the leaves and new-growth vines and curlicues, then let it dry completely.

Next, I sprayed on an acrylic sealer in a matte finish. It's important that the sealer be *sprayed*, not brushed on. A brush will pick up the crackling and ruin the piece.

Then, I used Antiquing Medium in a warm brown color. I coated it over the tabletop with a soft rag, then wiped off the excess with a clean rag to the shade I wanted and let it dry.

To finish, I rolled on a water-based satin varnish with a foam roller, applying three coats in all because the table would get heavy wear.

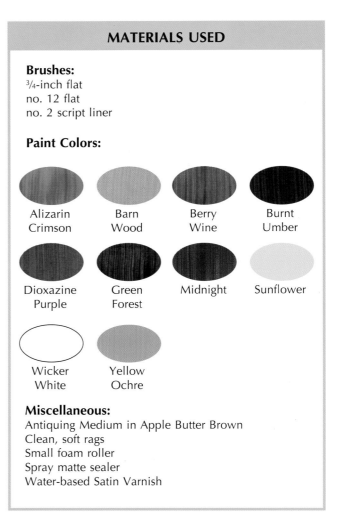

MATERIALS USED

Brushes:
¾-inch flat
no. 12 flat
no. 2 script liner

Paint Colors:

Alizarin Crimson · Barn Wood · Berry Wine · Burnt Umber

Dioxazine Purple · Green Forest · Midnight · Sunflower

Wicker White · Yellow Ochre

Miscellaneous:
Antiquing Medium in Apple Butter Brown
Clean, soft rags
Small foam roller
Spray matte sealer
Water-based Satin Varnish

Crackle Finish Step by Step

surface: painted wooden table

There are many types of crackling mediums on the market, including hide glues and other products people might suggest. But after the time spent on the old-world fruit tabletop shown on pages 100-103, I prefer to use FolkArt's Crackle Medium; it has always guaranteed success for me.

MATERIALS USED

Brushes:
¾-inch flat
Large house-painting brush

Paint Colors:

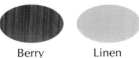

Berry   Linen
Wine

Miscellaneous:
Antiquing Medium
Clearcote Acrylic Sealer
Crackle Medium (Clear)
Large car wash-type sponge

---

1. Apply Crackle Medium

On an already basecoated surface, apply Crackle Medium with a ¾-inch flat brush or a foam roller, depending on the size of the piece. If you want your cracks to be bigger so more base-coat color shows through, apply a heavier coat. A thinner coat will produce finer crackling. Let the Crackle Medium dry.

The top of the wooden table shown here was basecoated with Berry Wine. But if you have an old mahogany piece that is dark and needs refinishing, it's better to let the mahogany show through rather than a base coat.

2. Brush on the Top Coat

Brush on the top coat with a large house-painting brush, being careful not to overlap your strokes. Overlapping them will lift the top coat, losing the crackling effect and making a mess! Stop your strokes at different lengths so the ends don't line up. The left side of the table shown in Step 3 shows what happens if the brush-strokes are overlapped.

3. Or Sponge on the Top Coat

Another quick and easy way to apply the top-coat color is with a car wash-type sponge for a finer, more random crackle. Lightly dampen the sponge, load your top-coat color and pounce the sponge, working quickly. Don't re-pounce in the same area. Let it dry, then spray on an acrylic matte sealer. (Don't brush on the sealer. That will lift the crackling and make a mess!)

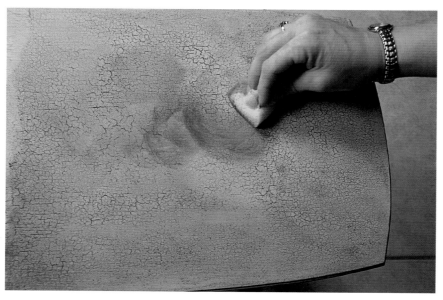

4. Finish with Antiquing Medium

If you wish, you can age your piece even more with an antiquing medium, which comes in several colors. Here I used FolkArt's Antiquing Medium in Apple Butter Brown. With a clean sponge dipped in Antiquing Medium, apply with a circular motion, then wipe off the excess with a soft rag. The more you wipe off, the lighter the color.

chapter 8

laundry rooms

Farm Garden Scene

surface: painted walls

Now just how exciting can a laundry room really be? Though laundry may be one of those chores we have to do, it doesn't need to be done in a dreary room. Painting a border of favorite flowers or a whimsical box of soap will help to brighten the gloomiest of laundry rooms.

The design used for the laundry room and connecting powder room shown to the right is a brightly colored vegetable garden scene with cute accessories, such as seed signs, a gardening hat, and a watering can with tomatoes painted on it.

The scarecrow is the focal point of the room. I drew its shape, then used a Butter Pecan wash for his face and hat, with Burnt Umber on the chisel edge of my brush to add texture to the hat. A thinned Berry Wine wash was sponged on for the shirt, which has a Berry Wine plaid painted on it with the ¾-inch flat. The pinstriping was painted using Sunflower on the script liner. Using the chisel edge of my large flat brush, I painted the straw on his neck, head, feet and hands with Yellow Ochre and Sunflower. I detailed his face with Yellow Ochre circles for cheeks, Licorice triangles for the nose and eyes and a big smile!

The pumpkins on the right side of the doorway were painted with Schoolbus Yellow and Pure Orange, and a little Naphthol Crimson for shading. The cabbages and celery were painted with a lot of Wicker White and a little Green Forest.

In the powder room, I sponged in the ground area using Maple Syrup and Green Forest. I also used a sponge, double-loaded with Maple Syrup and Wicker White, for the picket fence. Then I painted the turnips, carrots, onions and their green tops. Yellow daisies softened the white fence.

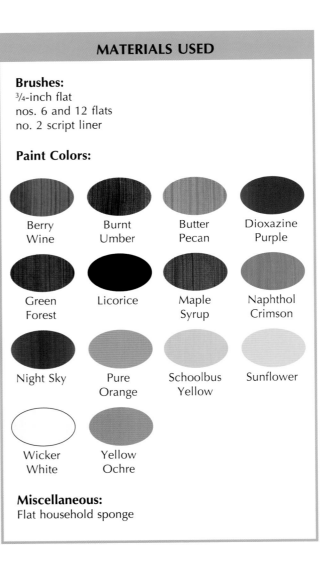

MATERIALS USED

Brushes:
¾-inch flat
nos. 6 and 12 flats
no. 2 script liner

Paint Colors:

Berry Wine | Burnt Umber | Butter Pecan | Dioxazine Purple

Green Forest | Licorice | Maple Syrup | Naphthol Crimson

Night Sky | Pure Orange | Schoolbus Yellow | Sunflower

Wicker White | Yellow Ochre

Miscellaneous:
Flat household sponge

Birdhouses and Roses

surface: painted wooden ironing board cupboard door (birdhouses)
painted wall (roses)

This laundry room was a homemaker's dream—spacious with lots of countertops and cabinets. The tall, skinny shape of the ironing board cupboard door seemed a natural place to paint some woodsy-looking birdhouses. And a vine of wild roses growing up and over the birdhouses helped fill the empty wall space and added color to an otherwise plain room.

I painted a mossy old urn on the left side of the cupboard door because it was the side that would be seen when entering the laundry room. Then, with the chisel edge of my ¾-inch flat brush, I painted light, airy vines growing up from the urn and arching over the birdhouses. Roses and rosebuds were placed along the vines, then the green leaves, finishing up with shadow leaves and curlicues.

Finally, to tie the painting in with other magnolia accents in the room, I painted a magnolia branch at the baseboard, adding the flower, bud and leaves lying over the baseboard. One last accent was a leaf falling to the ground.

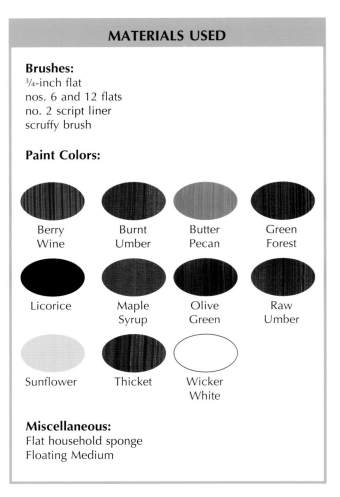

MATERIALS USED

Brushes:
¾-inch flat
nos. 6 and 12 flats
no. 2 script liner
scruffy brush

Paint Colors:

Berry Wine
Burnt Umber
Butter Pecan
Green Forest

Licorice
Maple Syrup
Olive Green
Raw Umber

Sunflower
Thicket
Wicker White

Miscellaneous:
Flat household sponge
Floating Medium

Trompe L'Oeil Window

surface: painted wall

Believe it or not, the open window and garden scene to the right is actually a perfectly flat wall. It was located at one end of a laundry room between a built-in desk and wall cabinets. The narrow horizontal wall space provided a perfect spot to paint something interesting. Usually a desk faces a blank wall and is covered with a mound of paperwork. A trompe l'oeil window was a good way to open up this enclosed space.

I measured out a wide window area, drew in shutters, painted them and all of the background scenery first and then painted the white of the window jamb. Next I focused on all of the details in the tree branch, birdhouses, fence, walkways and so on.

Then I concentrated on making the windows look as though one was open and the other shut by basecoating the frames and muntins in Wicker White. Using browns, I shaded in a windowsill, the molding and the grooves in the windowpanes. I finished by painting the magnolia spray to appear as though it was inside the window.

I usually do not put a sealer over my wall paintings. However, if your painting is in a well-used area, over a stove, near a sink or, as in this case, where the painting just looks flat, you may want to use a satin-finish sealer, which can be sprayed or rolled on.

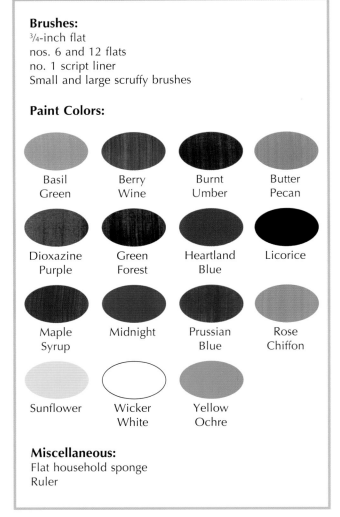

MATERIALS USED

Brushes:
¾-inch flat
nos. 6 and 12 flats
no. 1 script liner
Small and large scruffy brushes

Paint Colors:

Basil Green

Berry Wine

Burnt Umber

Butter Pecan

Dioxazine Purple

Green Forest

Heartland Blue

Licorice

Maple Syrup

Midnight

Prussian Blue

Rose Chiffon

Sunflower

Wicker White

Yellow Ochre

Miscellaneous:
Flat household sponge
Ruler

bathrooms

Venetian Garden

surface: painted wall in master bath

You may think that decorative painting a bathroom would be an ideal first project. However, due to limited working space, I think it may be one of the more difficult projects to attempt. You also must consider factors such as fixtures, flooring and tile that can't be changed without considerable cost, and whether or not your painted design can be viewed clearly and as a whole.

The master bath shown to the right had plenty of space in which to paint a design—it was a grand room in scope as well as feeling. The spa tub was nestled in a columned alcove with an Italian marble surround, and ornately framed mirrors overlooked his-and-hers vanities on both sides. The plaster walls were painted with a faux marble finish, subtly done so that it would not compete with the real marble in the room. Crystal chandeliers and brass fixtures added warmth and elegance.

Due to the moisture from the spa tub, a real framed painting in the tub alcove would eventually be ruined, so I designed a wall painting reminiscent of the real thing. The elaborate trompe l'oeil frame was painted with warm wood colors to match the moldings and echo the carved mirror frames on either side of the alcove. The whole effect was one of European grandeur.

On page 115, you can see how I painted the Venetian garden scene that added such beautifully subtle color to this room.

MATERIALS USED

Brushes:
¾-inch flat
no. 12 flat
no. 2 script liner
scruffy brush

Miscellaneous:
Flat household sponge
Floating Medium

Paint Colors:

Alizarin Crimson	Bayberry	Berry Wine	Burnt Sienna
Burnt Umber	Butter Pecan	Dioxazine Purple	Green Forest
Heartland Blue	Licorice	Midnight	Olive Green
Raw Umber	Salmon	Sunflower	Wicker White
Yellow Ochre			

Detail of Venetian Garden Scene

surface: painted wall in master bath

The back wall of the tub alcove shown on page 113 gave me a wonderful chance to design a trompe l'oeil painting that would look as if it had always been there. The homeowner wanted a feeling of looking out onto an old-world garden. We decided a Venetian garden, with ancient Roman columns and a splashing fountain, would fit the bill.

First, I painted the background building with maize-yellow tones, then worked forward, adding columns, trees, the fence, the old stone path and the fountain as the focal point. Then, starting at the back of the picture, I added very light, nondetailed wildflowers; the closer the flowers were to the foreground, the more detailed they became.

I added potted flowers along the walkway, including pink roses and creamy yellow snapdragons, plus vining roses over the arches.

To finish, I detailed the brick breakaways on the building, the design in the glass door, and all of the tiny vines and leaves over the columns, fencing and building. The splashing water was the final touch.

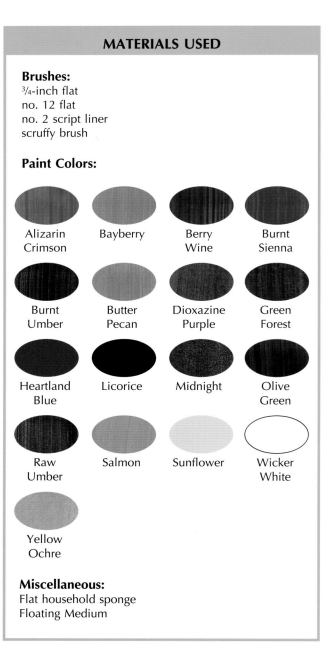

MATERIALS USED

Brushes:
¾-inch flat
no. 12 flat
no. 2 script liner
scruffy brush

Paint Colors:

Alizarin Crimson

Bayberry

Berry Wine

Burnt Sienna

Burnt Umber

Butter Pecan

Dioxazine Purple

Green Forest

Heartland Blue

Licorice

Midnight

Olive Green

Raw Umber

Salmon

Sunflower

Wicker White

Yellow Ochre

Miscellaneous:
Flat household sponge
Floating Medium

Birdbath in the Garden

surface: painted wall

Many master baths these days have large picture windows over the tubs, but there are other ways to bring the outdoors in. This bathroom had large, bare walls around the tub—just perfect for painting a flower garden with a birdbath.

The first design element was the leafy tree painted in the corner, with branches extending along both walls and a bird's nest perched on one branch. On the other side, I painted a latticework trellis with a pink rose vine growing up and over it as well as down and over the short dividing wall.

After placing the birdbath in the center, I painted a variety of birds, wildflowers and butterflies and a large yellow rosebush. For a bit of whimsy, I added a little bird splashing in the cool blue water of the birdbath.

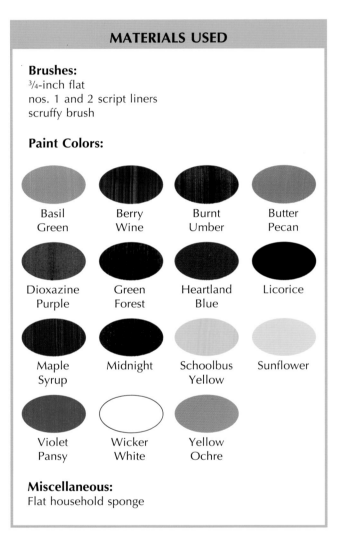

MATERIALS USED

Brushes:
¾-inch flat
nos. 1 and 2 script liners
scruffy brush

Paint Colors:

Basil Green

Berry Wine

Burnt Umber

Butter Pecan

Dioxazine Purple

Green Forest

Heartland Blue

Licorice

Maple Syrup

Midnight

Schoolbus Yellow

Sunflower

Violet Pansy

Wicker White

Yellow Ochre

Miscellaneous:
Flat household sponge

Basket of Wildflowers

surface: powder room walls

Powder rooms are often tucked under a staircase or somewhere where there's no natural light coming through a window. They can feel dark and shut in, even with a floral wallpaper meant to brighten things up.

The small powder room to the right had all of these shortcomings, but with an interesting sloped ceiling. A bright, cheery design painted on light ivory walls would help to open it up and give it a much airier feeling. I wanted to create the effect of being underneath an outdoor trellis supported by four corner posts.

In the four corners, I painted knotty, uneven treelike trunks for the posts, and wound grapevines up around those posts with a ¾-inch flat double-loaded with Maple Syrup and Burnt Umber. Along the tops of the walls, I painted full, twisting grapevines with Burnt Umber and Wicker White, following the line of the sloped ceiling, to look like dense foliage on top of the trellis.

Next, I painted a bird's nest in the grapevine, the large basket on the floor and the pot for the topiary all with Butter Pecan and Burnt Umber. I used the same mixture with a little Wicker White added for the body of the birdhouse.

I painted a morning glory vine on the topiary, and used my scruffy brush to pounce moss winding up the topiary and birdhouse poles. Wildflowers and greenery fill out the basket, and small rosebuds dot the vine trailing around the ceiling. A little brown bird looks curiously toward the framed picture on the wall, and a dried rosebud wreath adds a finishing touch.

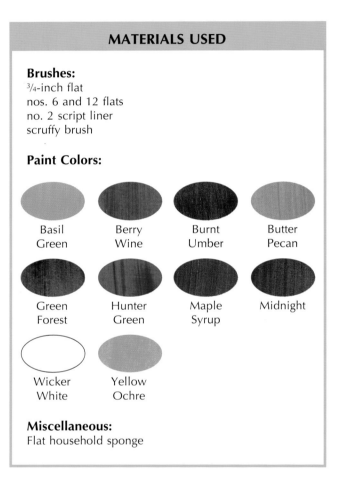

MATERIALS USED

Brushes:
¾-inch flat
nos. 6 and 12 flats
no. 2 script liner
scruffy brush

Paint Colors:

Basil Green

Berry Wine

Burnt Umber

Butter Pecan

Green Forest

Hunter Green

Maple Syrup

Midnight

Wicker White

Yellow Ochre

Miscellaneous:
Flat household sponge

BATHROOMS

Faux Marble

surface: wooden cabinet

Painting a faux marble finish is easier than you think and doesn't require a lot of specialized tools. I faux marbled the bathroom vanity to the right with just a household sponge, a ¾-inch flat brush and three colors of acrylic paint. The light green leaf design was added on top of the faux marbling for an extra touch of color.

The only tricky part to faux marbling is getting the veining to look natural. I studied many examples of real marble and practiced painting on scrap wood before I tackled my first project for a client. The key is to relax and not overdo the veining so it starts to look like tree branches. Keep a light touch.

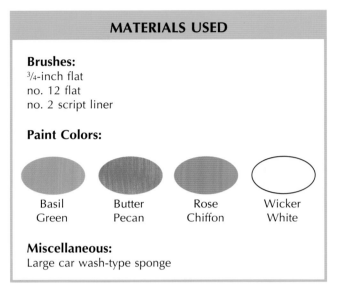

MATERIALS USED

Brushes:
¾-inch flat
no. 12 flat
no. 2 script liner

Paint Colors:

| Basil Green | Butter Pecan | Rose Chiffon | Wicker White |

Miscellaneous:
Large car wash-type sponge

Before
This is how the vanity cabinet looked before I began working on it—very dated and too rustic for this cream-and-rose tiled master bath.

BATHROOMS

1. Priming and Painting

First I primed and painted the wooden cabinet with a soft white latex interior house paint in an eggshell finish. While that was drying, I chose the faux marbling shades to complement the tile colors of the bathroom.

2. Sponging on a Darker Color

Using a dampened sponge, I picked up Butter Pecan and lightly streaked it diagonally, painting in the same direction on the doors, edges, stiles and rails.

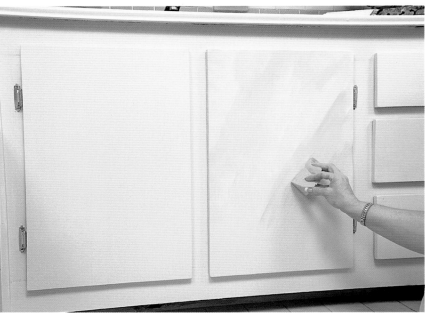

3. Beginning the Veining

With a ¾-inch flat brush, I thinned some Rose Chiffon with water and began painting a few veins of color in the same direction. I held my brush perpendicular to the surface and let the chisel edge of the brush do the work.

4. Adding Cross Veins

I loaded my clean ¾-inch flat brush with Wicker White and, staying up on the chisel edge, painted very thin cross veins, occasionally splitting the veins into Y shapes. Here's where studying real marble will come in handy because it's often the cross-veining that winds up looking stiff and unnatural. Remember, less is more. More veining can always be added, but it can't be removed.

5. Softening the Veining

I randomly blended some of the veins very lightly with a clean damp sponge to soften the edges and make them look deeper.

If a faux marble finish is enough, you can stop here. Spray on a matte or gloss acrylic sealer, let it dry and add new doorknobs and drawer pulls to finish.

I wanted to go on and paint a subtle design over the faux marbling, so I did not use a spray sealer at this point.

Compare this photo with Step 8. I think the delicate green acanthus leaves add a bit of elegance to the faux marble finish. What do you think?

6. Painting Pinstriping and Vines

Around the edge of the cabinet door, I freehanded some pinstriping with Basil Green and a no. 2 script liner. Then I added a curving vine with the no. 12 flat brush and Basil Green.

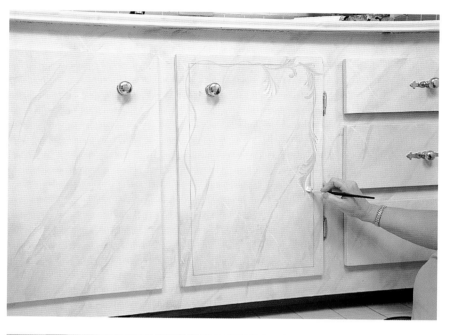

7. Painting Acanthus Leaves

With Basil Green and Wicker White double-loaded on a no. 12 flat brush, I used the chisel edge of the brush to pull the gently curving strokes of the acanthus leaves. Each stroke was a different length and slightly over-lapped the previous stroke.

8. Finish

The second door was painted the same manner, balancing the design of the two doors but not copying each stroke exactly. Then I adapted the design to fit on the three drawers, adding a few extra curlicues with Basil Green on the script liner.

Painted Tile Wall

surface: matte finish tile

In the same master bath shown on the previous pages, a large tile wall with a rose tile border served as the background for an open spa tub. I liked the acanthus leaves painted on the vanity cabinet so much, I decided to continue the design on this tile wall.

1. Painting the Outline
For this design, I studied Art Nouveau acanthus leaves. I used my no. 12 flat brush and Basil Green to lightly draw out the design freehand, counting out tiles to center the design within the border.

2. Layering Comma Strokes
I filled in the outlines with layered comma strokes using the ¾-inch flat brush, alternating Butter Pecan and Basil Green on one corner and Wicker White on the other.

3. Detailing the Acanthus Leaves
With Basil Green and Wicker White double-loaded on the flat brush, I painted the ruffled edges of the leaves and shaded the creases.

4. Finish
As done on the cabinet doors, I balanced the design on both sides without striving to match them perfectly. I didn't apply sealer to this wall because it will not be getting wet. However, if you want to paint inside a shower stall, you will need to use a glass-and-tile medium with your acrylics.

chapter 10

bedrooms

Pink and Blue Hydrangeas

surface: wooden furniture

Bedrooms are very flexible when it comes to decorating and design. You can find bed linens in an endless array of colors and prints, many of which are coordinated to drapes and accessories. Fabrics designed especially for bedrooms can be custom-made into comforters, canopies and curtains. Decorating themes are limited only by the taste and imagination of the bedroom's occupant. In short, bedrooms are great places to do some decorative painting!

Bedroom furniture lends itself especially well to being painted. You can find inexpensive pieces at auctions and yard sales, buy unfinished wood furniture or just refinish what you already have. Hand-me-downs can be freshened up with a couple coats of paint, or completely refurbished and customized to match a room's decor.

The furniture in the pretty yellow bedroom to the right was bought at a used-furniture store and was originally painted bright orange and green! But it was heavy, good quality, worth refinishing and, best of all, bought at a great price.

I repainted the whole set with hydrangeas to complement the custom-made comforter, headboard and canopy. Rather than copy the fabric's floral design, I adapted it to fit the shape and size of each piece and added my own touches of bluebells, tiny rosebuds and a rope-and-tassel motif. The soft yellow walls and white crown molding pulled it all together, making this a perfect room for a little girl to grow up in.

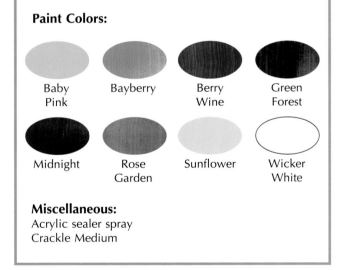

MATERIALS USED

Brushes:
¾-inch flat
nos. 6 and 12 flats
no. 2 script liner
3-inch nylon house-painting brush

Paint Colors:

Baby Pink

Bayberry

Berry Wine

Green Forest

Midnight

Rose Garden

Sunflower

Wicker White

Miscellaneous:
Acrylic sealer spray
Crackle Medium

Dresser

Pink and blue hydrangeas on a pale pink background—what could be more feminine? And the massing of flowers and bright green leaves helped the design hold its own against the strong florals of the fabrics. The dresser (above), the highboy and the bedside table (right) were all painted with hydrangeas, but the main bouquet and the details of each piece have slightly different looks. This shows that they were hand-painted, not mass-produced.

To create the delicate pink background, I base-coated each piece with Baby Pink acrylic paint and

let it dry. I then applied a heavy coat of Crackle Medium to make large crackles. The top coat of Wicker White was stroked on with a large house-painting brush. The pink base coat showing through the white crackling gives interest and depth, much more so than just a flat painted background.

I used Crackle Medium for this project, but, if you prefer, you can use Glazing Medium mixed with Wicker White acrylic paint to streak a wash over the pink base coat.

Highboy and Bedside Table

Once the crackled pink background was completely dry, I began painting the blue rope-and-tassel motifs along the edges of the pieces with a no. 12 flat brush double-loaded with Midnight and Wicker White. Then I laid out the design for the main bouquet, placing the big flowers first, then the smaller bluebells and finally the leaves.

Next, I painted all of the stems for the bouquet, lengthening the ones on the side panels of the highboy. With a no. 12 flat, I painted pink and blue hydrangeas, alternating Rose Garden and Berry Wine for the pinks and Midnight and Wicker White for the blues.

The bluebells and leaves were painted next, including the ones on the corner posts of the highboy and dresser. Finally, I added tiny pink rosebuds at the base of each piece, then used an acrylic spray sealer to protect against wear.

Faux Marble Columns and Door Crown

surface: painted walls

Master bedrooms often adjoin master baths and may or may not have a door or other architectural element to separate them. The master bedroom shown to the right was filled with wonderful antique furniture in dark or inlaid woods and a dramatic black carpet that extended into the bathroom. The doorway needed something equally dramatic, so I painted faux marble columns on either side with scrollwork detailing at the tops and bases. The columns helped to visually enlarge the doorway and soften the transition between the white walls and black carpet. They also framed the view into the bathroom, and the colors of the columns picked up the soft browns of the drapery beyond.

To paint the columns, I loaded the edge of one side of my dampened flat sponge with Butter Pecan and drew the sponge downward to form the rounded sides, then pulled some paint lightly toward the middle for the shading of the columns. With a ¾-inch flat brush side-loaded with Butter Pecan, I painted streaks of marbling in the columns and scrollwork details at the tops and bases.

The door crown below picks up the same colors and scrollwork used in the columns. I used a ¾-

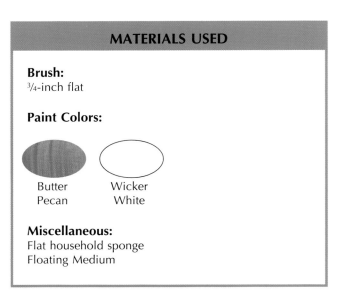

MATERIALS USED

Brush:
¾-inch flat

Paint Colors:

Butter Pecan   Wicker White

Miscellaneous:
Flat household sponge
Floating Medium

inch flat brush side-loaded with Floating Medium and Butter Pecan to paint the illusion of a sculptured crest over the doorway. I worked Floating Medium into my dirty brush (Butter Pecan) and misted in subtle shadows following the shape of the curves. These same accents can be used over baseboards, windows or pictures.

Raccoons on a Ladder

surface: painted wall

A child's bedroom can be fairly easy to decorate if you take your cues from the child's interests rather than trying to impose your own tastes. Children like to surround themselves with meaningful images more than just pretty pictures. The wall painting at right was based on a little boy's favorite bedtime story about a mom and dad raccoon.

To begin, I base painted in all of the larger shapes of the design. The stepladder was painted with a flat sponge side-loaded with Maple Syrup, then Burnt Umber was used for the steps and clay flowerpots. Mama raccoon's shirt is Yellow Ochre shaded with Burnt Umber, and papa raccoon's is Violet Pansy shaded with Night Sky.

Then I sponged on Quaker Gray and Wicker White for the raccoons' faces, detailing their eyes and noses with Licorice. Using a flat brush side-loaded with Licorice, I floated shadows around their features and hands, then painted the wild fur to add character. Mama raccoon's mouth is Berry Wine and papa raccoon's glasses are Yellow Ochre.

After all the green foliage was painted, I finished with the flowers—tall tulips of Berry Wine and Wicker White and yellow blossoms of Yellow Ochre and Wicker White.

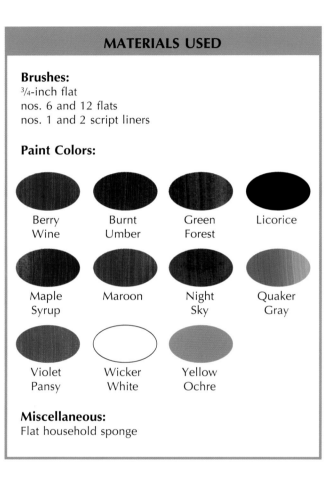

MATERIALS USED

Brushes:
3/4-inch flat
nos. 6 and 12 flats
nos. 1 and 2 script liners

Paint Colors:

Berry Wine

Burnt Umber

Green Forest

Licorice

Maple Syrup

Maroon

Night Sky

Quaker Gray

Violet Pansy

Wicker White

Yellow Ochre

Miscellaneous:
Flat household sponge

Pony, Horse and Dog

surface: painted wall

Children's bedrooms are great places for painting animals. To make realistic-looking animals, study pictures of your child's favorites and practice drawing them on paper. They need not be anatomically perfect, but they should have expressive faces that convey friendliness.

The trio of animals at right was painted for a boy who loves horses and, as you can see, his dalmatian, Domino, is also a big part of his life. So I created a doggie companion for the horse and pony. (*Hint*: If you want to re-create your child's pet as realistically as possible, take a slide of the animal and project it on the wall to make a tracing.)

After lightly pencilling the design on the wall, I used a flat sponge with Butter Pecan and a little Maple Syrup to base in the horse's and pony's bodies. I used a sponge with Wicker White and a little Maple Syrup to base in the dog.

To paint the horses' manes and tails, I used the chisel edge of my ¾-inch flat brush double-loaded with Maple Syrup and Burnt Umber. Licorice was used for their eyes, noses and hooves, with a little Wicker White for their foreheads and to highlight their eyes.

When the horse and pony were finished, I turned my attention to the dog. His spots were painted with Maple Syrup, his ears with Burnt Umber and his mouth with Rose Garden. I detailed his nose and eyes with Licorice and added a Heartland Blue collar. Finally, I sponged in the ground with Green Forest and Butter Pecan, and used the chisel edge of my flat brush to paint tufts of grass.

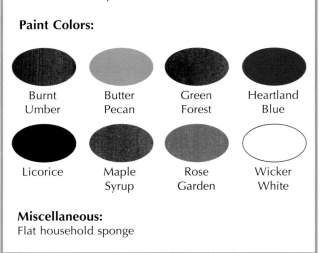

MATERIALS USED

Brushes:
¾-inch flat
nos. 6 and 12 flats
nos. 1 and 2 script liners

Paint Colors:

Burnt Umber · Butter Pecan · Green Forest · Heartland Blue

Licorice · Maple Syrup · Rose Garden · Wicker White

Miscellaneous:
Flat household sponge

Pink Rose Garland

surface: wooden window seat

Decorating a little girl's bedroom can be the most fun of all. Design choices are endless, and little girls usually have very definite ideas of what they want. Their hobbies and toys can serve as the basis for a room decor that reflects their interests and personalities—and their favorite colors!

A budding ballerina lives in this room, and there's no doubt about her favorite color. She and her mother had chosen a beautiful wallpaper border of ballet dancers in pink and lavender costumes. Then they found a floral bedspread in matching shades of pink, lavender and green.

The textured plaster walls were originally painted an off-white, which allowed me to sponge on two or three shades of pink to match the wallpaper border.

The paneled wood window seat had also been painted with a white semigloss. To warm it up, I used a flat household sponge and antiqued it with Butter Pecan, leaving more paint in the grooves of the molding to give an aged look. When that was dry, I painted a swagged garland of roses in each panel to complement the bedspread and to pull the room together.

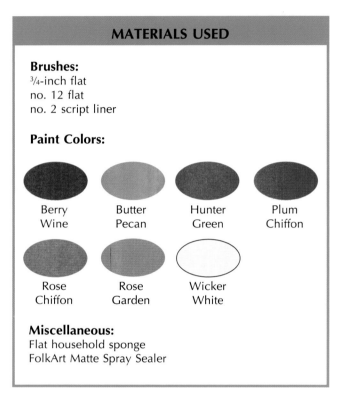

MATERIALS USED

Brushes:
3/4-inch flat
no. 12 flat
no. 2 script liner

Paint Colors:

Berry Wine   Butter Pecan   Hunter Green   Plum Chiffon

Rose Chiffon   Rose Garden   Wicker White

Miscellaneous:
Flat household sponge
FolkArt Matte Spray Sealer

Detail of Garland

For the window seat, I felt a swagged garland would help soften its angularity and the horizontal lines of the window blinds. After the wood panels were antiqued, I pencilled in a swag design on both panels to be sure they were even. Matching the colors to the bedspread, I painted the roses, alternating lavender between the pink-toned roses in each garland.

I filled in around the roses with the larger green leaves first, then smaller one-stroke leaves and finally very pale green shadow leaves. At each side, I draped ribbonlike vines from large green leaves in the corners, making sure not to copy the shape or placement of the leaves exactly.

After everything was dry, I used a spray matte sealer to protect against wear.

Trompe L'Oeil Shutters

The little dancer's bedroom also had a graceful arched window that looked out over flowering shrubs. To add interest to this already wonderful window, I painted open white shutters on the textured wall, shading them with Butter Pecan to soften their lines and make them appear three-dimensional.

The airy rosebud vines were painted to create the illusion that they were growing from outside the window in and around the shutters. The subtle green leaves match the ones on the window seat.

Ribbons and Roses

surface: painted wall

As a little girl grows into a young lady, ballerinas and dolls give way to slightly more sophisticated things. Bedroom decor can evolve, too, without spending lots of money on new furniture. Painted headboards are a great idea and the price is right!

The soft blue and yellow of this room's bedding inspired the colors of the painted roses and ribbon "headboard." I began by basecoating yellow into a faux fabric swag falling from the center, bishop's sleeves at the sides and puddling on the floor. I used a flat sponge to base in the colors and paint the folds and creases in the "fabric."

For the blue ribbons that match the bedspread, I used a ¾-inch flat brush double-loaded with Sterling Blue and Wicker White, and painted the large loops of the center bow and the trailing ribbon that wound around the swagged fabric. Then I painted four more bows that appear to be holding up the swagged fabric.

I used Rose Garden and Wicker White double-loaded on the ¾-inch flat to paint clusters of pink cabbage roses and buds, adding Yellow Ochre and Wicker White rosebuds and trailing flowers. Large and small leaves, vines and curlicues filled in the spaces.

I hung an antiqued plaster medallion in the center, but if you would prefer not to hang anything, try painting some vines trailing down from the center bouquet.

Doorjamb Dolly

As an extra accent in this bedroom, I painted a flower girl sitting over the corner of the doorjamb. The ribbons and roses on her straw hat echo the bouquets painted on the headboard.

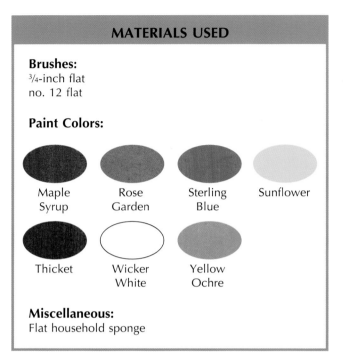

MATERIALS USED

Brushes:
¾-inch flat
no. 12 flat

Paint Colors:

Maple Syrup · Rose Garden · Sterling Blue · Sunflower

Thicket · Wicker White · Yellow Ochre

Miscellaneous:
Flat household sponge

index

Apples, 90-91

Basket of wildflowers, 118-119
Bathrooms, 112-127
Berries, 94-95
Birdbaths, 116-117
Birdhouses, 26-27, 108-109
Blueberries, 76-79
Bluebirds, 26-27
Brushes, 10

Cabbage roses, 64-65
Cabinets, 120-125
Columns, 36-43, 132-133
Cornices, 58-59
Crackle finish, 104-105
Cupboard for ironing board, 108-109

Dining rooms, 90-105
Dogs, 136-137
Doors, 54-71
Dressers, 130

Family rooms, 72-89
Family trees, 20-21
Farm garden scene, 106-107
Faux finish, 46-47
Faux marble, 120-125
Ficus trees in urns, 44-53
Fireplace screens, 82-83, 88-89
Floorcloth, yellow rose, 84-87
Floors, wood, 84-87
Foyers, 12-17
Fruit, 66-69, 92-93
Furniture, wood, 128-131

Garden carts, 24-25
Grand foyers, 12-17
Grapevines, 36-43, 66-69, 96-99

Hallways, 18-33
Highboys, 131
Horses, 136-137
House signs, 20-21
Hydrangeas, 70-71, 128-131

Ivy, 44-45, 58-59

Kitchens, 90-105
    walls, 66-69

Laundry rooms, 106-111
Lighthouse cove mural, 28-33
Living rooms, 72-89

Mantel, 72-73
Marble, faux, 120-125
Materials, 10-11
Medium, 11

Nests, 26-27

Old-world fruit table, 100-105

Painted walls, 18-33, 44-45, 64-65, 70-71,
    74-75, 80-81, 90-93, 106-111, 112-119,
    132-137, 142-143
Paints, 11
Palladian window, 74-75
Pine, unfinished, 88-89
Pink rose garland, 138-141
Plaster wall, 12-17
Plywood, unpainted, 82-83
Powder rooms, 118-119

Raccoons, 134-135
Ribbons, 64-65, 142-143
Rosebud border, 60-63
Rose garland, 72-75
Roses, 108-109, 142-143
Rose trellis, 22-23

Satin wall paint-based wood, 54-57
Shelves, wooden, 80-81
Stairways, 18-33
Subjects
    apples, 90-91
    basket of wildflowers, 118-119
    berries, 94-95
    birdbaths, 116-117
    birdhouses, 26-27, 108-109
    blueberries, 76-79
    bluebirds, 26-27
    cabbage roses, 64-65
    columns, 36-43, 132-133
    cornices, 58-59
    dogs, 136-137
    family trees, 20-21
    farm garden scene, 106-107
    faux finish, 46-47
    faux marble, 120-125
    ficus trees in urns, 44-53
    floorcloth, yellow rose, 84-87
    fruit, 66-69, 92-93
    garden carts, 24-25
    grapevines, 36-43, 66-69, 96-99
    horses, 136-137
    house signs, 20-21
    hydrangeas, 70-71, 128-131
    ivy, 44-45, 58-59
    lighthouse cove mural, 28-33
    marble, faux, 120-125
    nests, 26-27
    old-world fruit table, 100-105
    pink rose garland, 138-141
    raccoons, 134-135
    ribbons, 64-65, 142-143
    rosebud border, 60-63
    rose garland, 72-75
    roses, 108-109, 142-143
    rose trellis, 22-23
    trompe l'oeil, 80-81, 110-111
    Venetian garden, 112-115
    vines, 90-91, 94-95
    wall plaque, 22-23
    watermelon, 92-93

wisteria, 60-63
yellow rose floorcloth, 84-87
Supplies, 10-11
Surfaces
    cabinets, 120-125
    floors, wood, 84-87
    furniture, wood, 128-131
    ironing board cupboard, 108-109
    painted walls, 18-33, 44-45, 64-65, 70-71,
        74-75, 80-81, 90-93, 106-111, 112-119,
        132-137
    pine, unfinished, 88-89
    plaster wall, 12-17
    plywood, unpainted, 82-83
    satin wall paint-based wood, 54-57
    stained wood, 58-59
    textured walls, 34-43, 44-53, 60-63, 94-99
    tile, 126-127
    varnished wood, 72-73
    walls, 12-17, 18-33, 34-43, 44-45, 44-53,
        60-63, 64-65, 70-71, 74-75, 80-81, 90-93,
        94-99, 106-111, 112-119, 132-137
    wood, 54-57, 58-59, 72-73, 100-105

Tables
    bedside, 131
    old-world fruit, 100-105
    painted wooden, 76-79
Textured walls, 34-43, 44-53, 60-63, 94-99
Tile, 126-127
Trompe l'oeil signs, 80-81
Trompe l'oeil windows, 110-111

Varnished wood, 72-73
Venetian garden, 112-115
Vines, 90-91, 94-95

Wallpaper, 69
Wall plaques, 22-23
Walls, 34-53
    kitchen, 66-69
    painted, 18-33, 44-45, 64-65, 70-71, 74-75,
        80-81, 90-93, 106-111, 112-119, 132-137,
        142-143
    plaster, 12-17
    textured, 34-43, 44-53, 60-63, 94-99
    tile, 126-127
Watermelon, 92-93
Windows, 54-71
    palladian, 74-75
    trompe l'oeil, 110-111
Window seats, 138-141
Wisteria, 60-63
Wood, 100-105
    floor, 84-87
    furniture, 128-131
    pine, unfinished, 88-89
    plywood, unpainted, 82-83
    satin wall paint-based, 54-57
    stained, 58-59
    varnished, 72-73